PROBLEMS OF PLANNING
EAST AND WEST

PUBLICATIONS OF THE INSTITUTE OF SOCIAL STUDIES

SERIES MAIOR

VOLUME XV

INTERNATIONAAL INSTITUUT
VOOR SOCIALE STUDIËN - 's-GRAVENHAGE
1967

PROBLEMS OF PLANNING

EAST AND WEST

by

RUDOLF BIĆANIĆ

MOUTON & CO · THE HAGUE

1967

Printed in The Netherlands by Mouton & Co., Printers, The Hague

PREFACE

This is a collection of lectures on planning given at the Institute of Social Studies in The Hague between 1963 and 1965.

The first and longer part, *Problems of Planning: East and West*, deals with the forms and methods of planning action according to the environment in which planning takes place, the actors involved, the aims pursued and the instruments used. The original lectures have been brought up to date by the inclusion of such materials as the British National Plan, the French Fifth Plan and the Soviet Reform of October 1965.

The study is mainly based on analysis of the official documents of some 25 countries, and to a lesser extent on their interpretation by planning theorists.

The second part deals with the monocentric and polycentric approaches to planning. This is a theoretical introduction to the morphology of planning, and there is particular discussion of polycentric type planning as opposed to monocentric. I consider that problems connected with polycentric planning are the most important and challenging that planners face today and hope that this study will be a contribution in a field where too much has not yet been written.

The third part of the book is an essay which resulted from a discussion on the role of computers, and whether they have a centralizing or a liberalizing function.

I wish to express my thanks to the Institute of Social Studies in The Hague for publishing these essays, and to the Center of Advanced Studies in the Behavioral Sciences at Stanford, where I had the opportunity to edit some parts of them and revise and rewrite many others. I am most gratefully to the members of the staffs at The Hague

Institute and the Center who helped me prepare this manuscript for publication, particularly to Miss Miriam Gallaher and Mrs. Joan Warmbrun of the Behavioral Sciences Center.

RUDOLF BIĆANIĆ
Zagreb University

Center for Advanced Study in the Behavioral Sciences, Stanford, California
January 1966

CONTENTS

PART II: ON MONOCENTRIC AND POLYCENTRIC APPROACHES TO PLANNING

PART I

PROBLEMS OF PLANNING – EAST AND WEST

INTRODUCTION

There are so many concepts and methods of planning that a simple dichotomy, centrally planned vs. free market economy, is out of place. Modern economic development continually reveals new avenues for planning. Are trends converging or diverging? It is difficult to give a straight answer for such a complex activity as planning; the answer would be in many ways yes, in some no.

But an answer can only be given after as wide as possible an analysis of planning. To present a complete typology would not only be too ambitious, but would impose for the moment too rigid a classification. Instead we shall try to rationalize the process of planning by giving some typical examples.

The term planning itself is not quite unanimously agreed upon, and the definitions run from very general ones concerning decisions about future activities to very complex ones embracing many dimensions. Our definition would be: Under planning we understand institutionalized, and rationalized, *ex ante* quantified socio-economic development, over definite periods of time, carried out by deliberate human activity, on a certain area, and using instruments chosen in advance, with the purpose of achieving economic gain by balancing resources with requirements.

In our analysis we have followed the Max Weber – T. Parsons – J. Tinbergen model of economic action at its simplest, which distinguishes three elements in each economic action:

(1) The Actor (2) The Aims (3) The Instruments

To these three elements we have added a fourth: the environment, and we are beginning our analysis with this element.

I. THE ENVIRONMENT

Planning means action. This action does not take place in a vacuum, but always in a certain social, political, economic, and ecological environment. This environment is neither neutral nor passive to planning action, but reacts to it in different ways, strengthening or weakening the action, presenting obstacles to it, and requiring specific methods for different situations.

Five main groups of problems will be considered in connection with the environment: (1) the level of development, (2) planibility of economic activities, (3) the institutional framework of the economy, (4) government and private planning, (5) concentration and planning.

The environment in planning, i.e., the immediate medium in which the planning action is exercised, is the economic process. Planning interferes with this process in one way or another, changing its spontaneous, i.e., "non-planned", course.

A. PLANNING AND THE LEVEL OF ECONOMIC DEVELOPMENT

The first problem to deal with here is whether planning is an economic activity that can take place at any level of economic and social development, or whether a certain level of development is necessary before planning can be introduced as an economic activity.

There is little doubt that Soviet planning theory assumes planning can be introduced into an economy only when it has achieved a certain level of economic development. This assumption is based on Marx's well-known theory of socio-economic formations, and Lenin's application of this theory to the development of the U.S.S.R. The line of thought runs thus: Socialism is a socio-economic formation which follows capitalism and therefore can be established only on the basis of highly advanced productive forces, attained during capitalism when it has already reached its peak development and is decaying because it cannot develop the production forces further. Planning an economic process is the socialist method of further organizing these forces in order to surpass capitalism. Lenin's contribution to this theory was significant. Starting with the Marxist theory of development he asked himself and his followers what was to be done after the political revolution led by the bolsheviks had been successfully carried out in the underdeveloped and backward Russian empire. The dilemma was whether to propagate capitalism and let it develop the productive forces of the Russian empire to the level where socialist planning would take over, or to retain political power and use the rebuilt state machinery to develop the productive forces which would grow faster under the dictatorship of the proletariat than under capitalism. In this latter way a sufficiently high level of productive forces would soon be developed.

Today, too, Soviet theoreticians still hold that planning can take place only at a certain level of economic development.[1] A definite opinion prevails that the plans of the underdeveloped countries should be distinguished from national planning of the Soviet type. The reason put forward is not only the institutional one, which we shall consider later, but also the level of economic development.

The Soviet Union began to employ overall planning in 1929, more

[1] "The social character of the production process forms the material basis of planning, its first premise. Small scale production without constant connections among economic units, without division of labour and specialization cannot serve as a basis for planning. Small scale production has not yet developed into social production, and labour spent in various economic units has not yet become part of aggregate social labour."

"The possibility of planning within the framework of a national economy is created and developed only on the basis of a developed production process with a social character, and linked to it a process through which production processes are merged into a unified social production process. This process occurred in the period of the industrial revolution in the bosom of capitalism. Its material basis was large scale mechanical industry, but the process was squeezed into the framework of private property and did not make use of the enormous possibilities which were being opened up." N. A. Tsagolov, ed., *Kurs polititcheskoy ekonomii* [Treatise on Political Economy] (Moscow, Academy of Science USSR, 1963), pp. 109-110.

"Certain possibilities for economic planning can be seen in countries liberated from imperialist oppression. ... These plans should not be mixed up with the plans of socialist countries. They do not embrace the totality of the national economy ... but only a small in volume state capitalistic sector. These plans are not compulsory for private enterprises and serve in the main the interests of the national bourgeoisie. They represent a form of state capitalistic regulation of the economy." M. G. Kolodny, A. P. Stepanov, *Planirovanie narodnogo hozjajstva SSSR* [Planning the National Economy of the USSR] (Kiew, 1962), p. 16.

than eleven years after the revolution of 1917. Three remarks can be made in connection with this Soviet theory of planning:

(a) Definite criteria in concrete quantified terms as to when the actual level suitable for planning takes place had never been laid down. This level could either be identified with the beginning of "social production", in the sense of modern industry with a high level of concentration of labor and indivisibility of capital, and with a highly integrated market economy, or it could be considered as the level of economic development of a monopolistic economy where liberal *laissez faire* can no longer operate successfully.

(b) The Soviets started to plan in their most underdeveloped central Asian areas at the same time as in the most developed western Soviet republics. Here the explanation was given that underdeveloped areas can plan their development when linked to the more developed parts of an economy. There is no doubt that this theory applied to the people's democracies of Eastern Europe after the Second World War had a very unfavorable effect on their planning and development, a fact that is now openly admitted.

(c) Around 1948, planning in Eastern Europe started in all countries by almost identical Stalinist methods. Emphasis was laid upon institutional changes rather than on the level of development, which, on the whole, was somewhat higher than the Soviet level of development in 1917, and at least in two cases was considerably higher (Czechoslovakia, East Germany).

Nevertheless the developmental factor plays a great role in efforts to organize joint planning on an international scale in the CMEA, where differences in methods of planning between the more developed and less developed socialist countries cause considerable problems (e.g., in Roumania).

The countries of Eastern Europe had a period of some years before they started on their first national plans. The Chinese communist government ignored the problem of developmental preconditions for planning, and started their first plan in 1953, only four years after their revolution.

In Yugoslavia the concept of developmental preconditions for planning has been different. In fact, one of the main points of contention with the Soviet leaders before 1948 was that they advised the Yugoslav government not to start with national plans but to have a transition period of reconstruction of war damages and losses. The Yugoslav government's point of view was different and the first five-year plan started in 1947, two years after the revolution. Instead of following the

Soviet government's advice: "First reconstruct, then plan", they took the opposite view: "Plan the reconstruction and carry on into the development of the socialist economy." In recent years differences in the level of development of the six Yugoslav republics are causing many planning problems.

The opposite view as to the level of economic development where planning can take place is expressed in the well-known American theory of planning of W. W. Rostow.[2] Planning should be used to launch the "take off" in economic development, and last until the period of self-sustained growth is reached. Here again developmental and institutional requirements for planning are mixed.

(d) There should be public planning to supplement the very weak or even non-existent private *entrepreneurship* and carry on until the *entrepreneurs* gain experience and accumulate sufficient capital to take over the leadership from public planning. This substitution of the planning mechanism by the mechanism of the firm is sometimes called a theory of neo-mercantilism.

(e) Planning should provide the mechanism by which accumulation of capital can be achieved in order to serve and complement private investment by public means until a self-sustained level of development is attained. Public resources have to be used particularly to build the infrastructure of the economy.

(f) Planning should supplement and expand undeveloped and atomized local markets until such markets are developed. Then overall free competition delivers better results than the public planning mechanism.

(g) The link with the world market should be the first field where planning is necessary, expanding the economy with the help of foreign aid and compensatory financing. Thus developmental planning should

[2] The American theory as expressed by Rostow accepts planning (or better to say, national programming) for the earlier stage of economic development, and rejects planning for the later developmental stage. Planning is identified with the action of government, and the main justifications for planning are the following: (a) because there are no efficient private *entrepreneurs*, needed when the economy sector develops rapidly; (b) at an early stage, when production is simple and able to meet the simple and comparatively homogeneous needs of the population, planning is possible, but when in the course of development production becomes diversified, it is dificult to manage it by a state bureaucracy which lacks competent experts; (c) industrial and agricultural activities are best managed when private individuals or firms compete with each other and are forced by competition and not by planning to achieve maximum efficiency, when accounts reflect true costs and output is responsive to the changing tastes of the people. W. W. Rostow, "The Roles of State and Private Enterprise", *American Economic Report* (American Embassy, London, Nov. 1963).

have a built-in foreign aid element; this attitude has sometimes been criticized as neo-colonialism (e.g., by the Chinese communist authors).

Moreover, planning of some sort on a multilateral basis is encouraged, even demanded, from outside in order to improve and rationalize the economic policy of underdeveloped countries. Just to mention a few examples of such induced planning: Marshall Aid was linked with the obligation of the receiving countries needing assistance for redevelopment to plan the increase of their income by fifty per cent in ten years. O.E.C.D. activity which resulted from Marshall Aid still operates on the same, though somewhat watered down, assumptions. The World Bank demanded that the newly liberated African countries plan their resources in relation to the credits received, and extended this to a demand for the preparation of a plan for overall development. The Alliance for Progress in America also demanded that the receiving countries produce ten-year national plans for their development.

Such a public planning mechanism should last until taken over by the capitalist market and a firm mechanism. When this level of development and of institutional change is reached, planning will no longer be necessary.

Comparing the attitudes of both theories as to the development of the environment of planning, one could say that the American theory uses the planning *ad quem* (up to) approach while the Soviet theory stands on the planning *a quo* (from) basis. The American concept would employ planning until the level of capitalist development is reached, whereas the Soviet starts with planning from the level where the capitalist system has been developed. The one asserts that planning is justified up to a level of development where economic interdependence can be achieved by the market mechanism, and that this mechanism can operate by using separate and isolated instruments as determinants of growth policy without combining them into a consistent set, a plan. The other, the Soviet theory, maintains that the determinants of economic development can be put together into a consistent set only when a certain level has been reached where this set becomes necessary for further development. Before that level no planning is possible; only particular instruments can operate successfully in economic policy.

It seems as if the two, between them, combine to leave a planning vacuum in which the market mechanism operates under the liberalistic conditions of non-existent perfect competition. Yet both theories are confronted with the fact that developed and developing countries on many different levels of economic development actually do plan. This also opens the question whether conventional measurement of the level of economic development is adequate when dealing with conditions of planning.

It goes beyond the scope of this essay to discuss what actual level of development is necessary for planning. In our opinion it cannot be measured by one-dimensional economic growth alone, i.e., gross national product per head over time. A definition of at least three-dimensional growth needs to be applied, growth in height, i.e., of capital per head, growth in width, i.e., increase in economic interdependence, and growth in depth, i.e., the quality of the economy, that is the productivity of labor and of capital, including the effects of technical progress.

The problem of the level of development did not appear to be an obstacle in the planning of developed countries. The Netherlands, Norway and France, Italy and Sweden have all shown that planning can be carried out at their high level of development, and that it is useful and to a degree successful. It is estimated that the rate of growth of the French economy has increased by one per cent per year thanks to planning.

Recently some other most developed countries, e.g., Great Britain, have revised their ideas about planning in order to achieve faster economic development.[3] Thus the developmental approach has increased in importance.

In developing countries the level of development has often not been taken into consideration. The limiting factor in planning was considered to be, at the utmost, to what extent any action could be carried out by the administrative mechanism. The reason was that the concept of planning was, and still is, used very indiscriminately to cover everything from the drafting of projects for government policy to the implementing of long-term physical urban plans. The preconditions for planning were considered mainly from the angle of the requirements of the governmental or administrative mechanism as a substitute for the "normal" *entrepreneurial* activity (normal in the scene of a developed country) in order to speed up the economic process. In spite of their hand-to-mouth life and overstrained conditions, countries at a low level of development ventured to plan. The reasons are varied: domestic political pressure; a weak capitalist class of *entrepreneurs* unable to carry out the task of

[3] The first national plan for 1966-70 in Great Britain was presented to the Parliament by the Labour Government in September 1965. *The National Plan*, Cmnd 2764, HMSO (1965). Its main motto is "Working for prosperity". It aims at a 25 per cent economic growth over 5 years; it is officially stated that "such an increase is within the nation's capacity".

development; the urge to develop fast for reasons of political competition; anticipations aroused as to the results of growth by drawing an image of what things would look like when the plan was fulfilled; rationalization to avoid waste and duplication of effort – all these have led to planning with different degrees of success in spite of low levels of development.[4, 5]

B. THE DEGREE OF PLANIBILITY IN TECHNOLOGICAL OR FUNCTIONAL SECTORS

Not all economic activities are equally suitable for planning. They are planible to a different degree. Under planibility we understand the objective technological or functional qualities inherent in certain economic activities which make them suitable for planning. Technological processes such as a great concentration of the factors of production, depending on their indivisibility; quick technological changes requiring faster capital depreciation; the time required to change mass production patterns and products; introduction of new products onto the market; increasing interdependence of production in certain industrial branches, etc., all mean different degrees of planibility. Thus planibility depends on certain functional economic factors.

It is easier to plan manufacturing industries than agriculture; grain production than livestock farming; basic industries with homogeneous and slow-changing types of products (e.g., electricity) requiring a comparatively small number of decisions than light industries of consumer goods, requiring great changes in kind, quality, and types of products. It is easier to plan the activity of the banks and financial institutions which deal with what is in fact a very homogeneous article – money – than to

[4] For evaluation of planning in Asian countries see UN-ECAFE, *Economic Survey of Asia and the Far East*, 1961, p. 35. ss. For African countries compare UN-ECA, *Economic Bulletin for Africa*, II, 2 (1962). For all developing countries see: UN, *Planning for Economic Development*, Parts 1 and 2 (New York, 1965); UN, *Development Plans: Appraisal of Targets and Progress in Developing Countries* (New York, 1965); *World Economic Survey*, Part I (1964).

[5] We may take Ghana as an example. The level of development has explicitly been taken into account in the new Ghanaian seven-year plan (1963-1970). The first development plan of 1951 was partial, and after independence in 1959 a new plan was prepared but postponed until 1963. The growth process started with the building of infrastructure and social services. This has achieved satisfactory progress and established the necessary preconditions for planning accelerated growth. But at the same time it has created problems of disequilibrium between

plan the physical production of goods. Thus planibility, depending on technical qualities, has a definite influence on planning policy. On the other hand, it is also affected by exogenous factors such as weather and climate, foreign trade, political changes, etc., which may all have different effects on planning.

It is not accidental that in the Soviet Union general planning started first in electricity (GOELRO plan for the electrification of the Soviet Union in 1920), which was to be developed on a basis of a very homogeneous product, electric energy. Natural resources were to follow. Least effective was, and still is, planning in agriculture, which is restricted to the planning of compulsory or commercial deliveries of products, largely leaving aside the planning of production proper. Planning of consumer goods not only lagged behind but also proved to be the least successful in fulfillment, both in quantity and in quality of goods and with regard to satisfaction of consumer wants.

In the non-socialistic countries the first field where planning took place was that of financial policy. Spending the government budget, allocation of the credits of public financial institutions for developmental purposes, and planning the use of foreign currency were, and still are, the instruments of planning policy most used. Direct planning of physical production is in most cases extended first to planning of transportation (railway and road building) and of electricity as the most planible activities.

Planning is most widespread in transport because of the heavy capital coefficient and the great indivisibility of capital. Next comes industrial development, while the impact of planning is least extensive in the retail trades and in industries producing consumer goods, where it is most difficult because of the variable tastes of customers. Agriculture presents special difficulties, particularly the planning of current production, for there risks are the greatest and decisions on the spot most numerous. On the other hand, the problems of agriculture are the most fundamental problems of economic development in underdeveloped and developing countries.

In the agricultural sector planning is most obvious in credit policy, in administrative price fixing, ceilings and subsidies, and in public works such as land reclamation and irrigation, last in the line is planning of current crop production.

---

the rates of growth of social services and of physical output, increasing dependence on foreign sources and chronic unemployment. Thus a drastic shift is planned from infrastructure and social services to agriculture and industry.

C. PLANNING AND THE INSTITUTIONAL FRAMEWORK

The theory of Soviet-type planning maintains that only socialist countries can plan. The two principal questions here are: What is a socialist economy? And: What is planning? In Soviet planning theory the institutional definition dominates, and planning is considered to be possible only for countries where private property has been abolished and socialist property introduced. The identification of planning and socialism has been taken over by some adversaries of socialism who, in rejecting socialism, reject planning as well (Hayek, von Mises). The opinion of the Soviet planning theorists so far has been that planning can operate rationally only where the private proprietor of the means of production has been removed, and the property subjected to the will of central planners.[6] Consequently the main condition of planning is considered to be institutional change culminating in the nationalization of the means of production. This is seen as creating the environment necessary for planning in order to allow the most rational application of conscious human action to economics.[7]

This reasoning carries the implicit assumption that the owner of the means of production is their operator-manager. But the equalization of the function of owner = operator = manager = capitalist has undergone many changes.

The separation of the function of management from that of ownership

[6] A recent Soviet book on planning emphasizes this point of view: "Planning of the national economy takes place at a certain period of social and economic conditions; dictatorship of the working class; social ownership of the means of production and socialist socialization." M. G. Kolodny, A. P. Stepanov, *Planirovannie narodnogo hozjajstva SSSR* [Planning of the National Economy of the USSR] (Kiew, 1962), pp. 5-6.

[7] It is interesting to note that while the Soviet economists emphasize that planning is possible only in a socialist society, nevertheless at present some reserves are made. These are of a dual character. On the one hand, they speak of the gradual character of planning and distinguish the simpler and more complex forms, finding simpler forms of planning in the whole history of society in each form of cooperation of labor. The antagonism between the planned character of work within the enterprise and the anarchy in social production, since the industrial revolution, is emphasized. On the other hand, planning on the general scale of the national economy is contingent on the existence of one center of control in the production process; thus planning reaches its limits at the boundaries of the State, i.e., it goes as far as the power of the center can reach. Here two things are left out: one, that refers to the nationalization of the *most important* means of production only (leaving others aside), and the problem of international planning for socialism as a world economic system where there is not one center of authority. Cf. Tsagolov, ed., *Kurs politicheskoy ekonomii* [Treatise on Political Economy], Tome II (Moscow, 1963), pp. 111-113.

in the modern capitalist economy is of major importance for planning, as planning is more concerned with the function of management than of ownership. The separation is developing to an increasing degree even in the monopolistic capitalist economy, and in the socialist economy it is complete. There is little doubt that this fact is now widely recognized and that even in Soviet theory there is some realization that planning is possible in capitalist countries.[8]

Legal property relations are not the only obstacles to the mobility of people and products. There are many other environmental obstacles which prevent the human will from achieving a rational planning of resources. There is the immobility of the irreproducible natural resources which require special methods of spatial horizontal planning. There is the indivisibility of productive forces as expressed in size of plant and equipment, from technological norms and blocks of investment up to macro-economic problems of balanced versus unbalanced growth. There is the relative immobility of the labor force and of agglomerations of consumers in large settlements, with investments in urban dwellings. The historical environment also plays a very important role as expressed in invested, fixed capital, the existence of firms, factories and services as already going concerns. Another obstacle of a purely institutional character is the constitutional frame of the state organization, frontiers of states, regions, local administrative and political units. These are all immobilizing factors, and vested interests of all kinds may be expressed, such as national loyalties, local patriotism, and also bureaucratic conflicts of competence. Instead of applying pure, rational criteria to economic activities planning must be adjusted to existing immovable obstacles.

Such problems are known in all areas under consideration. Greater allegiance to local interests than to wider loyalties, nationalism, regionalism, separatism, the isolationism of government departments – these are phenomena restricted to neither capitalist societies nor to planning in socialist countries where the principle: "To each according to his work", does not stop at the factory gates but is being extended to regions and states as well.

However, the institutional factor plays a great role even within the Soviet planning system. The whole ramification of the planning mechan-

[8] The success of planning methods in some developed countries in Europe, especially the Netherlands, the Norwegian and most recently French planning, has led to the recognition among Soviet authors that planning is a method sucessfully applicable to such countries much more than was previously believed.

ism follows the institutional structure of the Soviet Union: planning is done by the federal government, the Soviet Republics and the local authorities each having their own planning centers and plans. When decentralization was introduced in 1957 and the regional Economic Councils were established, these were larger than most of the republics but none of the republics was dismembered so that it fell among different Economic Councils. The same principle is kept with the more recent higher Economic Councils.

The institutional factor is evident in agriculture where planning in *kolkhozes* is different from that in the state farms. The Eastern European countries followed the same pattern as the Soviet Union, in a more standardized way. In the late forties they copied the latest stage in the development of Soviet planning methods, taking them for the final and absolute truth. When they gained experience they began to develop their own methods of planning, and the consequence in the early sixties was the adoption of the principle that each country has to find its own way to socialism – which also refers to planning. The result has been an ever increasing variety of methods and instruments of planning, and these institutional factors are now causing great difficulties in the international planning of CMEA.[9] Most of the Soviet planners hold that planning is not possible in capitalist or in underdeveloped countries for institutional reasons, private property being the main obstacle to planning. This is the generally accepted view of Soviet planning theorists, although some admit (S. G. Strumilin) that private planning does exist when they describe the advantage of public as against private planning, private planning being limited by the sphere of the private property of individual firms.

However, recent discussion regarding the position of the enterprise in

[9] All Eastern European countries are engaged in building socialism, and they started from a Stalinist model of planning. They show a similar general tendency to change this, mainly by introducing better scientific methods of planning, coordinating of macro- and micro-plans, liberalization of enterprises from administrative ties, strengthening enterprises in their striving toward profitableness, and stimulating every worker to get interested in improvement of the work of the enterprise he works in. But each of these countries does these things by different planning instruments (taxes, premiums, cost calculations, etc.) so that the comparative prices become quite difficult if not impossible to assess, and there is no market to show them. V. P. Miroshnichenko, ed., *Planirovanie v evropeyskih stranah socializma* [Planning in the European Countries of Socialism] (Moscow, 1962). So instead of an international socialist planning agency, a socialist international bank was created in 1963 in Moscow to do the coordinating activity more on a business than on an administrative line, a very significant change of outlook.

the Soviet economic system has shown a considerable change of view. Demands are more and more often heard that the enterprises should have a more autonomous position, that the market be liberated from administrative ties and the planning of the enterprises relieved from petty administering and ordering about "by telephone from 300 miles away".

In Yugoslavia the institutional change in the management of socialist enterprises, switching them from the administrative system to that of workers' management, has also brought forward institutional changes in planning. Enterprises secured the right to make their own autonomous plan within the framework of the social macroplans, the latter setting parameters of behavior for the enterprises on the market but not setting quantitative targets for them in absolute magnitudes.

D. GOVERNMENT AND PRIVATE PLANNING

The institutional factor also plays a great role in the planning of non-socialist countries. There is little doubt that in many of these countries planning is extended only to the government sector. The larger the government sector the more planibility there is. Thus planning activity coincides in varying degrees with the range of organizing, regulative, and operational activity of the state.[10]

[10] The Japanese Five-Year Plan is based on the private enterprise system which gives a free rein in planning to private enterprise as much as possible and restricts direct control measures by the government to the minimum; the government uses indirect methods such as dissemination of the contents of the plan to the public, as well as fiscal, banking, trade and foreign exchange policies. However, it is stated that there is a limit to the voluntary adjustment power of private enterprise, and that therefore it is necessary for the government to take appropriate measures to realize the plan. This is particularly the case: (a) for basic industries, (b) for those things which are difficult for private enterprise to carry out such as the building of roads, railways, port facilities, public facilities for industrial centers, etc., (c) for improvements of the sewage system, parks, and other environmental services as well as construction of homes for those in low income brackets, (d) for promotion of education, especially scientific education, and compilation of elaborate economic statistics. Economic Planning Agency, Japanese Government, *New Long Range Economic Plan of Japan*, 1958-61, pp. 18, 19.

Introducing the Fifth French Plan, P. Massé characterized the relationship between the micro -and macro-planning as follows: "The will to invest of our enterprises has above all to assure the industrial development of our country. It is linked to the anticipations of the market demand and of profits, and also to the requirements of modernization derived from international competition. This will be encouraged by the perspectives of expansion set by the Fifth Plan, and

In these cases planning is identified with the administrative planning of government activities, limited to general government agencies and those under government control, financed out of the state budget or public financial institutions. and confined to the state or public property. In some countries the government sector has been expanded into a public sector including some other activities such as public agencies, municipal and communal services, or local self-government. Where nationalized industries exist they are either treated separately as a special sector, included in the business sector, or put into the government sector. The first is the case in Norway, the second in the United Kingdom, and the third in France. In other countries cooperation between the private industrial sector and the public sector has taken the form of organized cooperation where industrial representatives have either a consultative voice, or the right to take the initiative. Typical is the case of France where there is a "constant dialogue" between the government and the business organizations. In Britain this dialogue has taken a more institutionalized and more formalized procedure than in France, establishing 20 economic development committees.

E. CONCENTRATION AND PLANNING

The third main environmental problem is that of *concentration* of industry with regard to planning. It is considered that only large corporations can make use of plans, while planning is not necessary, or even useful, to small scale industries, or to small family holdings in agriculture where it is indeed taken to be impossible because of the great number of decisions which have to be made instantly on the spot. Thus where there are no large corporations there can be no planning. These widely accepted views can be questioned at least insofar as they concern macro-

---

by the confirmed intention of the Government to defend its objectives." *Le Monde*, 31 July 1965.

This is clearly expressed in the British national plan: "Our economy, like most others in the modern world, is a mixed one. The Government element is important; public spending is a large part of total expenditure; for this reason the Government must raise large sums in taxation; a large part of the basic industry of the country is carried on by public corporations; the Government are able to exercise authority in many other fields. All this gives the Government great economic power and influence. They intend to use this to secure faster growth and national solvency . . . ." "Both Government and industry have to plan several years ahead and it is desirable to coordinate the forward estimates of both." *The National Plan*, pp. 2, 3.

economic planning based on the law of great numbers. Nevertheless, there are complaints, at least in France, that it is the big monopolistic corporations and the large oligopolies that are the main beneficiaries of planning. They can have an adequate staff for planning, they know how to use national plans for their particular interests, and can influence the macro-economic planning decisions and make a profit from them.[11] In the Netherlands, Sweden, and Great Britain, large corporations show the greatest interest for planning.

Two different policies are envisaged to meet these dangers. One is to abolish planning altogether, and the other is to create institutions which will put the planning process under democratic control and make use of it for the benefit of the whole population.[12]

Socialist planning left entirely to the state, means the predominance of the state bureaucracy in its hierarchical order, with all the problems which machinery of such kind involves, marrying administrative centralization to business centralization: i.e., big enterprises to the central

[11] Indicative planning works most effectively in highly concentrated sectors of the economy, where the need to plan ahead has been accepted by the firms themselves, such as iron and steel, chemical and mechanical industries, electric machinery, etc. M. Maclennan, "French Planning, Some Lessons for Britain", *PEP*, 1963, p. 342.

This planning method was strongly criticized by F. Perroux: "Monopolies in France and Europe are gaining in strength. They create both supra-normal profits and innovations. The plan which develops them and depends on them cannot at the same time attack them. It does not possess the means to discriminate between their positive and negative effects." F. Perroux, *Le IVe Plan Français* (1962), p. 22.

[12] In America views as to the feasibility of planning in a free enterprise economy are divided. W. W. Rostow maintains (a) that the private sector in no way need divert resources away from the objectives laid down in a national plan. "In the United States, Western Europe and Japan we have seen that a massive private enterprise sector can keep within the bounds of a common interest and in fact be an essential reinforcement to it." The opposite view is expressed by A. Berle: "The pluralist economic system ... operated by several hundreds of large corporations cannot plan a national economy ... large corporations oppose planning because it limits or reduces their own power of decision." From this approach the French economist Perroux draws the following conclusions: "these words denounce the opposition between the development plans of large private units of production, and the plans of national development. They admit that in the present state of political and social structure neither the rulers nor their administration can substitute their decisions for the decisions of large production units, nor can they arbitrate effectively in their decisions. Economic growth and the composition of the national economy are the result of competition among the large private corporations. They are not the consequence of a structural preference established by a political arbiter in the name of general interest." W. W. Rostow, *The Roles of State and Private Enterprise, op. cit.*, p. 11; A. Berle, "La grande entreprise", *Encyclopédie Française*, IX, pp. 9, 10, 5; F. Perroux, *Le IVe Plan Français*, pp. 108-109.

government, and the small ones to local government.[13] The remedy being applied for this is to extend planning by making it a democratic process, to democratize the whole planning procedure. Workers' management is one method to attain this, polycentric planning is another.[14]

[13] This attitude has remained dominant throughout Soviet planning. "It is impossible to conceive effective leadership without the existence of one single leading center whose duty is to be responsible for the development of the branch (of industry), for the unified policy of technical improvement, for an advanced organization and effective production, the right location and the rational employment of labour and technical cadres." "Mazurov Report", *Pravda*, Oct. 3, 1965.

[14] Workers' management was first introduced in Yugoslavia in 1950 and it led necessarily to further changes in the methodology of planning, such as making of autonomous plans by the enterprises, indirect planning by setting up of parameters, market mechanism as part of the planning procedure, and finally self-financing investment in socialist enterprises.

II. AIMS OF PLANNING

Since planning has been introduced in countries with differing socio-economic and political structures, the plans have different aims. We can distinguish these aims by content, by the finality of goals aimed at, by the choice made between several aims, and by the degree of compulsion involved.

A. PLANNING AIMS BY CONTENT

Plans may be classified into four categories according to the content of planning aims:

(1) Planning aims as technique.
(2) Planning with politically neutral aims.
(3) Planning with political extra-economic aims.
(4) Planning aimed at changing the social structure.

1. *Planning Aims as Technique*

Under this heading we put the aims of planning defined from the point of view of the technique used to rationalize the economic process. Planning aims are set as the result of statistical laws, being "aimless" extrapolations. Objectives are set in a formal way, with little regard to content, without asking the question in whose interests the aims are set, who are the actors and what the instruments, in what environment the plan is to be applied.

The authors of this kind of planning consider planning as rationalized action of the economic man on a higher level. If economics in general are "about scarce resources", then economic planning ought to be conrerned with more consistently economizing and rationalizing the use of scarce resources.[1]

[1] To some French planners the plan represents "economic organization" on a higher level, whose task is to reduce "the unknown and the mystical" (C. Gruson)

In the plans we have analyzed we have been able to find the following formulations of aims in this kind of planning, which we give in brief:

(a) Planning is every kind of decision making for future action (W. Eucken), thus planning is exhausted in forecasting.

(b) Planning is the technique of business management [2] extended to the field of public economic policy, e.g., following the slogan: What is good for big corporations should also be good for the state, i.e., micro-economic planning turned macro-economic. There are people who successfully practice planning on the enterprise level and oppose it on the national level. Others reason: Why should national affairs be managed less rationally than private business affairs?

(c) The opposite of this concept is that which says: The aim of planning is to extend the procedure of public administration to economic activity. Administrative planning of the Stalin type is an obvious example.

(d) The aim of planning is to do "generalized market research". This formula of French planners extends the methods of market research to plans which are considered as substitutes for the market.

(e) The aim of plans is to operate as "reductors of uncertainties". Minimization of risks on a micro- and macro-scale is supposed to be the aim of plans in all instances.[3]

(f) The aim of plans is to "provide a framework for different policies" of government.[4] This can also be extended to a concept of a concerted economy where planning is to provide a platform and a machinery for dialogues between business, trade unions, and government departments.

2. *Planning Aims as Politically Neutral Aims*

The second group of planning aims comprises those objectives of plan-

---

and to introduce intelligent participation, norms of economic discussion, and division of burdens, accepting the economic cost which has to be paid for the existence of multiple decision centers.

[2] The word planning has different meanings. In one general sense, it means the planning (planification) of the national economy; in the other, narrower sense, as used in the U.S.A., it is defined as rational management of the functioning of the enterprises.

[3] The most recent book of P. Massé discussing French planning has the title: *Le Plan ou l'Anti-hazard* (Paris, Gallimard, 1965).

[4] The aim of the Greek plan is to give a "constant framework for different types of economic policy" (1959-63). Greek delegation, National and Regional Economic Planning in Greece. W. Isard, J. H. Cumberland, "Regional Economic Planning", *OECD*, pp. 41, 22.

ning which are considered politically neutral.[5] They consist of economic constraints put on developmental decision making in optimization of economic activity. No ideological aims are involved and no political constraints acknowledged.[6] Of course this does not mean that political aims or ideological prejudices are not implicitly involved, but only that they are not explicitly acknowledged.

Here we can find the following formulations of aims of planning:

(a) Optimal allocation of resources.

(b) Full employment of labor.

(c) Full use of the capacity of production.

(d) Maximization of the standard of living, or of potential welfare.

(e) Maximization of economic growth.

(f) Achievement of balanced growth, or of general dynamic equilibrium in the national economy.[7] It is also formulated as an economic law of keeping the right proportions (in the U.S.S.R.).

(g) The ironing out of economic cycles. Thus one planning aim is to inaugurate a consistent anticyclical policy.[8]

[5] Neutrality in the income policy was expressed in the French Fifth Plan: "... as the norms of the plan have an indicative character, desired by the majority of those concerned, and such method is solely compatible with the freedom of discussion of wages and salaries; this situation has evidently as a counterpart that the Government which have imposed nothing can guarantee nothing." This is particularly so as a policy of reciprocal contracts between parties engaged was not accepted.

[6] Planning in the Netherlands is based on excellent forecasts which shortened the operations of the planning period so much that the recent editions of the Central Bureau of Planning deny the plan even the character of a plan, putting the term in inverted commas. Nevertheless the plan consists of measures in economic policy taken or announced, having a retrospective and a prospective part based on some well founded assumptions, and resulting in careful forecasts of some macro-economic (only) magnitudes, such as general economic indices, production capacity, distribution and spending of income, and capital market situation. "Netherland Central Planning Bureau", *Central Economic Plan 1961*, p. 10.

[7] The purpose of the Swedish plan is to create an "image" of the economic future, to inspire confidence and give information indicative of fiscal monetary and commercial policies, to facilitate general targets by its large macro-economic forecasts, inducing private firms to adjust their plans to the general targets of the national plan (on national aggregate and sector levels). I. Svennilson, R. Beckman, "Long-term Planning in Sweden", *Skandinaviska banken*, 3 (1962).

[8] While developing countries concerned mainly with the change of their economic structure do not deal with the problem of business fluctuation, the Japanese plan is very much concerned with it. It underlines that the plan must try to prevent excessive fluctuations, to reduce their amplitude to the minimum, make possible stable development and stabilize the economy. "Economy Planning Agency", *New Long Range Economic Plan of Japan*, p. 12. The British plan states: "Periodic crises have led to sharp checks to economic expansion and pro-

3. *Planning with Political Extra-Economic Aims*

Under this heading we put those aims of planning which are not politically neutral but are directed towards certain political objectives explicitly included in the plan by exogenous factors. In such instances economic variables are put under extra-economic constraints. Therefore this may be called teleological planning. Not economic but extra-economic gains are maximized. Costs are minimized only to the extent that extra-economic aims permit. The aims of planning here are:

(a) Planning of national defense, or rearmament.

(b) Planning in a war economy, both military and civilian.

(c) Planning to achieve national unity, to build national states or to build a socialist economy based on autarchy.

(d) Planning to achieve the general social interest where the plan is considered as a social contract, as a materialization of the *volonté générale* of J. J. Rousseau in economics.[9]

(e) Planning to achieve social harmony on the basis of existing economic relations rectifying abuses in order to preserve uses. Another example is when the objective of planning is to put a ceiling on workers' wages, or to combat inflation, etc. in order to preserve vested interests.

(f) Planning to win the competition between different social systems, or between different blocs of states. An example of this is provided in planning the growth of the U.S.S.R. economy in order to reach and surpass that of the U.S.A., or in the U.S.A., to speed up the rate of growth in order not to be caught up to by the Soviet Union. Another example is that of the United Kingdom, which is introducing planning in order to match the rate of growth of France or the Federal Republic of Germany.

(g) To this category belongs another set of planning aims: that of planning as a demobilizing factor in respect to the masses of the population. Lenin said that "the plan" represented the will of millions of people

---

ductive investment ... it is the Government's aim to break out of this vicious circle and maintain policies which will enable us to enjoy more rapid and more sustained economic growth." *The National Plan,* p. 1.

[9] J. Åkerman, "Theory of Industrialism", *Causal Analysis and Economic Plans* (Lund, 1960), p. 219. B. de Jouvenel, "Planning in France, techniques and lessons", *Moorgate and Wall Street Review* (New York, Fall, 1961), p. 24.

The increase in investment expressed carefully in the French Fifth Plan "is due to the will to invest by the enterprises and the will to save by the Nation". These wills are converging, and the expression of these wills goes beyond financial dispositions and develops a frame of moral contract between the productive activities and the Nation. *Rapport général sur le Ve Plan.*

united for one single purpose. Similar formulations can be repeatedly found in many other plans.

4. *Planning Aimed at Structural Changes*

Planning an economy is planning a society. This is true to a considerable extent whether it is done consciously or not. The fourth category of planning aims deals with changing the society by economic planning or what amounts almost to the same, planning social changes.

These are the most obvious cases of aims towards changing the social structure:

(a) Direct *developmental* aims of economic planning which involve structural changes, e.g., industrialization. This refers not only to changes in the magnitude of variables or in their parameters. The whole economic model is in question, with the aim of changing its structure and mechanism.[10] Another coordination system has to be set up, following the

[10] The last Italian Five-Year Plan explicitly states that its main aim is not to preserve the socio-economic structure by establishing a dynamic equilibrium of the present set of existing determinants of the development of the society, but to serve as an instrument of economic and social change by selecting complexes of determinants which are defined in their time, and in technical and instrumental dimensions.

"In this framework (of the Five-Year Plan) economic policy must be directed not to crystallization of the social and economic structure but to determine changes which are useful to the interests of the collective. ... The programmation assumes the function of an instrument which, in a dynamic and unitaristic vision of Society, makes a coherent selection of objectives of economic social progress and a common obligation to follow it in time, in modes, and in necessary instruments." *Il Piano economico quinquenale 1964-68*. Exposé of the minister A. Giolitti, Jan. 9, 1964.

The British plan expressed the demand for change in the following way: "To make the plan work requires above all an acceptance of change. For the manufacturer, changes in what he makes, what he sells and where he sells it; for the worker, changes in what he does, where he does it and how he does it; and for all of us a different approach to prices and incomes. Change will often mean disturbance and we must take care of the effect it has on the individual. But without change there can be no opportunity and no reward." *The National Plan*, p. A2. Change is also emphasized in the French Fifth Plan; a profound change "as a new type of expansion based on an appropriate dosage of dynamism and restraint". The Plan is preoccupied with the dilemma: expansion-stability which it intends to solve on a higher level of development. This change involves the transformation of the industrial apparatus because industrial development is the guarantee of national independence and social progress." This has to be obtained by increased expenditure on fundamental and applied scientific research, by employment lifted to a higher basis of technical training and by use of the science of decision making based on a network of information. The third objective is the policy of increasing exports.

The aim of the Greek Five Year Plan is to "establish a coherent policy aiming process of transformation. This aim also involves changes in the whole socio-economic structure of the society.

(b) Direct *institutional* change taken as a planning aim which also leads to changes in economics. E.g., planning land reform as an instrument for the abolition of the feudal or tribal structure of society leads to planned effects in the whole economic structure. This is particularly the case in countries where national liberation from colonial rule is taking place. Here political planning and institutional change elicit a different set of economic objectives, which have to be stated as planning aims.[11]

(c) The aim of *mastering the influence of monopolies* through economic planning is one which involves political risks that have to be planned also.[12]

---

at mastering the structural obstacles which prevent the country from developing economically." This program fixes objectives of growth considered mutually compatible, establishes a program of investment, and defines an administrative monetary, financial and social policy which the government has the intention of carrying out in order to achieve the general objectives. Ministère de finance, Royaume de Grèce, *Mémorandum sur la programme de développement économique de la Grèce* (Athènes, 1962).

The Ten-Year Plan for Ceylon is another developmental plan with the objectives: to provide employment and reduce unemployment; to achieve equilibrium of the balance of payments; raise the standard of living; diversify the economy; attain equitable distribution of national income. "National Planning Council", *The Ten-Year Plan* (Colombo, 1959), p. 60.

The Charter of Punta del Este envisaged development programs such as "comprehensive and well-conceived national programs of economic and social development, aimed at achievement of self-sustained growth, carried out in accordance with democratic principles". These are in fact plans of economic development. R. Prebisch described such a plan as a "well coordinated group of efforts whose aim is to expedite growth, or maintain it at the same rate if this is already high, to make it as steady as possible and to improve the distribution of income. Planning and government intervention are not necessary to maintain the existing order of things, but to transform it in an orderly and rational way". J. C. Dreier, ed., *The Alliance for Progress. Problems and Perspectives*, 1962, pp. 57, 60, 123, 131 ss.

11 The objectives of the seven-year perspective plan in Ghana are: (a) to ensure employment for everyone joining the labor force, at a high level of productivity and with a rising standard of living; (b) the colonial structure of production to be completely transformed; (c) the new structure of production must enable the country to play its full role in a Pan-African or at least a West African economic community; (d) government participation must ensure its socialist policy of distribution and utilization of the national income. "National Bank of Egypt", *Economic Bulletin*, No. 1 and 2 (1963), p. 117.

12 The British plan, on one hand, follows a policy of encouraging greater competition in order to make the economy more dynamic and efficient by technical progress; on the other hand, it accepts that structural changes take place through mergers. *The National Plan*, pp. 48-49.

(d) The most ambitious aims to attain socio-economic structural changes are in plans which intend to change a whole *society*. Planned social changes by building socialism is the aim expressed in several plans, although in different ways.[13]

[13] The Soviet twenty-year general plan has very ambitious aims; development which will bring the USSR to lead the world in productivity per head; (a) the greatest productivity of labor in the world; (b) increase of production of material goods to satisfy all the wants of the Soviet people; (c) gradual transformation of socialist production relations into communist production relations; (d) victory over capitalism in economic competition, and national defense capable of repelling any invader.

"Yugoslavia's present social plan established the basic proportions of social production and distribution, taking into consideration, within that framework, the free initiative of economic enterprises under prevailing market conditions and certain regulatory measures taken by the state. ... The main stress of direct intervention by the central social and state bodies should be solving the structural problems of economic development and securing general conditions for economic stability, preservation of the unity of the system, equal conditions for economic activity and stability of rights ... permanent assistance to the economically underdeveloped parts of the country.

"The planned economy ... should insure the maximum possible liberty for the individual in the production and consumption of goods. In this sense freedom of initiative by the socialist producers and citizens represents an incomparably greater economic force and higher consciousness than does capitalist private initiative. ... It is precisely for this reason that socialism in economic competition with capitalism must emerge triumphant." *The Programme of the Yugoslav League of Communists*, 1958, pp. 159-160.

The second Indian Five-Year Plan stated: "The task ... is not merely to get better results within the existing framework of economic and social institutions, but to mould and refashion these so that they contribute effectively to the realization of wider and deeper social values. These values or basic objectives have recently been summed up in the phrase 'socialist pattern of society,' i.e., the basic criterion must not be private profits but social gains, in greater growth and greater equality of incomes and wealth. ... The accent of the socialist pattern of society is on the attainment of positive goals, the raising of living standards, the enlargement of opportunities for all, the promotion of enterprise among the disadvantaged classes and the creation of a sense of partnership among all sections of the community."

The Third Indian Five-Year Plan: "through democracy and widespread public participation, development along socialist lines will secure rapid economic growth and expansion of employment, reduction in disparities in income and wealth, prevention of concentration of economic power, and creation of the values and attitudes of a free and equal society." Government of India, *Third Five-Year Plan*, 1961, p. 9.

The Five-Year Plan for the U.A.R. stated its aims thus: "... increasing of the rate of national economic development, and speeding up production in all economic activities in a balanced, integrated and complementary way which leads to a continual increase in the national income and to diminish enormous inequalities of personal wealth and income and ensure the contribution of all individuals, by their efforts and funds, towards the development of national resources and their utilization in raising the standard of living, in fortifying their

B. THE FINALITY OF AIMS

As we have shown, there is a great variety of planning aims and many devisions under which they can be classified. In fact there is quite a hierarchy of plans which can be aligned from many different angles, as to their priority in time, their importance, their administrative hierarchical order, planibility, etc.[14]

Here we wish to emphasize one specific classification related to the importance of plans from the point of view of their aims. In this respect we shall divide all aims of plans [15] into four groups:

(1) ultimate ends, (2) general objectives, (3) perspective goals, and (4) operational targets.

1. *Ultimate Ends*

Under ultimate ends of plans we mean those ends which express in some way the philosophy, the political or ideological ideals, and desires of the planners, their final aims.[16] These aims are put in indefinite terms, so

---

own dignity and integrity and in building a democratic socialist and cooperative society in which both public and private capital cooperate for the interest of all parties." U.A.R., *General frame of the 5-year plan for economic and social development, 1960-1965*, P.V. VI (Cairo, 1960).

The ultimate objective of the new first Seven-Years Development Plan (1963-1970) in Ghana is the building of a socialist economy. The process of socialization may take some twenty years, in which period a mixed economy will be maintained with the public sector gradually achieving domination.

[14] The French Fifth Plan made a clear distinction between the previsions and objectives of the plan; as the latter were not guaranteed, both were subject to revision, which cast some doubt as to the firmness of the planned equilibrium. This uncertainty was strongly criticized by the Economic and Social Council. They said that it reduced the Plan to a study of the market; to an aggregate of government directions of economic policy, which could be discarded at will. Furthermore, the subordination of the uncertain Plan to the fixity of the budgetary imperatives made them state that in fact the Budget was the Plan, and demanded considerable changes. Representatives of all three trade union centers – the Socialist, the Communist and the Catholic – also rejected the project of the Fifth Plan after their project of a counterplan and their amendments were voted down in the Council. Also the representation of the agricutural interests disagreed with the government project of the Fifth Plan.

[15] We are trying to introduce a distinction in these terms. Aim is used as a general term, while end, objective, goal, and target are more specific and progressively more concrete in meaning. Thus we can talk of ultimate ends, general objectives, perspective goals, and operational targets.

[16] While some authors underline that the French plan has no ultimate aims and that ideological discussions never preoccupied the planners, P. Massé, General Commissaire of the Plan, put the final aims of the plan in the following terms: "to prepare a stage of coherent development on the lines suggested by the preferences of the Nation," these preferences being: to improve the living conditions of

that their final implementation is not limited in time. Nor can it be exactly quantified and represent a more or less precise tendency towards certain ultimate aims. They give the "image", create the inspiration or form the atmosphere of planning, the spirit of the plan.

Some plans do not specifically mention such aims. The reason may be that they are not known by the planners or that the planners did not think it necessary to mention them. Sometimes the planners want to be "realistic", and thus do not mention such ultimate aims for they may only create unnecessary controversy for the actual planning period, during which they will not be fulfilled in any case. Or sometimes the planners have never put to themselves the question of the final ends of their planning action, consciously or unconsciously avoiding the issues, preferring to present their plans as politically or ideologically neutral. A similar approach is that of assuming that the ultimate ends underlying planning are accepted by general consent, tacitly agreed upon by everybody, and therefore it is not necessary to mention them. They are assumed not to be controversial.

Nevertheless one should not underestimate the mobilizing force of such ultimate aims for the masses of the population, who have to make efforts to implement them. For this reason we may also call such aims *metaplanning* aims. There is no doubt that in many plans there are concealed or assumed but not explicitly stated final aims of plans.

2. *General Objectives of Plans*

Plans stretching over long periods of ten, fifteen to twenty years are usually called *general* plans. We can call their aims general objectives of planning, comprising a rather small number of indicators put in very general terms. Nevertheless such planning objectives are usually quantified and limited in time, still within the reach of scientific methods of forecasting. At present there are not very many such general plans; most are still supposed to serve as working hypotheses and are not promulgated as official plans.

3. *Perspective Goals*

Perspective goals are often employed and vary in their aims. Their time dimension marks three to ten years of the planning span. But their main

the people by increasing purchasing power, particularly for the less favored sections and regions; qualitative improvements; reassessment of the industrial civilization; bias towards increasing investment in collective services; to determine the true interests of the Nation, not confusing them with its wishes, which have to be decided by the Nation in its political bodies that must make final choices.

characteristic does not lie in merely their time dimension (medium-term plans). The quality of their targets is such that they give a comparatively small number of composite indicators for a small number of aims, thus providing ample scope for choosing different variants not precise enough for direct action. These are also called "plans of plans", since they serve as the basis for making operational plans. The aims of such plans are stated in various ways.[17, 18] Soviet Five- and Seven-Year Plans are plans of this nature, as are many plans of similar duration.[19] There is both

[17] The Turkish Five-Year Plan states that its main purpose is to "attain a balanced and speedy development for Turkey within the democratic system, approved by the Grand Assembly." This plan ought to express "a desire for planned development as well as preferences for a higher standard of living in Turkish society."

[18] The five immediate objectives in the Seven-Year Plan in Ghana, which show an increased maturity of economic judgment, are: the substitution of domestic products for imports; the expansion and modernization of building materials production; the processing of agricultural and mining products (so far exported); introduction of basic industries in a small way; industrial development compatible with that of other African countries. Within these objectives the priorities are set for the public sector in the following order: maximum utilization of existing plant capacity; expansion of existing enterprises in preference to creating new ones; completion of projects in process of construction; creation of new industries. "National Bank of Egypt", *Economic Bulletin*, 1963, No. I. 2, pp. 110-118.

[19] The Soviet aims of planning in the Seven-Year Plan are put in the following way: (a) building of the material and technical basis for communism; (b) continuous increase of the level of national consumption; (c) a higher degree of social planning in organization for optimal utilization of natural resources and increase of the productivity of labor; (d) coordination of development and proportionality, by removing disproportionalities; (e) rational location of productive forces; (f) building of reserves for continuous economic growth; (g) strengthening of the national defense. For discussion of this, cf. S. Khrushchev, *On Controlling Figures of the Development of the National Economy of the USSR in 1959-1965* (Moscow, 1965). In 1965, the aims were changed to a certain degree. "The most important condition for the use of the advantages of the socialist system is the perfecting of planning and of management of production; increase of economic stimulation of industrial enterprises and of their rights in operational activities." "Mazurov Report", *Pravda*, Oct. 3, 1965.

The system is gradually being changed under the pressure of developmental factors. The plenary meeting of the Central Committee of the Communist Party of the USSR in September, 1965, introduced the following reforms of the Soviet system of planning: increased role of perspective planning; the basis for planning should be the 5-year plans for both state plans and plans of enterprises. This should give them the possibility of successively incorporating into production the achievements of science and technique; secure continuous specialization and cooperation in production, and enable them to introduce new products. Great emphasis was put on the reintroduction of centralized planning methods, through one single state plan which must be unquestionably fulfilled; at the same time a continuous development of the initiative of the enterprises is proposed which will use the system of economic stimulation instead of the adiministrative one, which economic and political-psychological reasoning behind the determination of goals for such perspective plans. The psychological reasoning is based on the assumption that the period of the perspective plans is of such duration that living adults can expect to see the results of the plans fulfilled in their own life time, and that the changes that occur during such a period will be such that the differences will be noticeable enough to justify the additional efforts and sacrifices for the gains achieved. Economic reasoning follows the estimated length of the investment cycle, or the average harvest (one very good, one very bad, and three average years). A third type of reasoning is based on the methodology of planning. The perspective period is such that it gives the planners enough time in later years to correct any mistakes made in the early period of

---

was hitherto predominant. This incentive aimed at stimulating the material interests of the workers, at the use of prices, calculations and profits.

The project of the Yugoslav Seven-Year Plan had the following objectives for the 1963-1970 period: (1) further development of socio-economic relations by developing self-management in production and all other activities which strengthen the position and the role of the working man, which means an accelerated material production and an increase in the level of labor; (2) increasing satisfaction of material and cultural wants of the working people; (3) an accelerated and harmonious increase of production on the basis of existing capacity, and the building of the necessary new capacities of production which have their justification in the existing and other natural conditions; (4) as fast as integration as possible of the Yugoslav economy into the international division of labor on the basis of comparative costs; (5) more harmonious regional development, and the harmonious growth of the under-developed republics and areas, the employment of the increase of active population and of surplus agricultural population.

The principal objective of the Japanese Five-Year Plan is to provide for a steady increase in the standard of living and full employment by achieving the maximum rate of growth consistent (which is significant) with economic stability. The objectives are as follows: (1) economic growth to match the population increase and employment of those agriculturally and industrially underemployed; (2) expansion of exports; (3) increase in capital accumulation; (4) reinforcement of basic industries, such as strengthening transportation, particularly roads and highways, energy, and the consolidation of the industrial areas of the country; (5) boosting the industrial structure to a higher level; (6) modernization of the structure of agricultural production; (7) improvement of the employment situation and living standards; (8) increased role of public finance and banking. "Economic Planning Agency", *New Long Range Economic Plan of Japan* (Tokyo), pp. 12-17.

The new Italian Five-Year Plan enacted by the Center-Left Government makes a distinction between permanent and specific aims of the plan. The *permanent* aims are the following: economic development, high level of employment, equilibrium of the balance of payments, and stability of prices.

This policy has to assure a better distribution of the national income in order to overcome the structural, zonal, and social disequilibria. It has to assure maximal growth and a better quality of the economy in such a way that the problems of Italy can be attacked with a vision of the whole and on the basis of precise priorities of importance and urgency. *The specific* objectives of the Plan the perspective plans. The law of great numbers operates in cases where there are at least five elements at stake in the set. Thus the sum of five yearly plans is not necessarily equal to one perspective five-year plan.

4. *Operational Targets*

Operational planning targets are concrete targets which are well defined as to time, space, instruments, and actors. They form the basis for actual action and are expressed in quantified and predicted magnitudes with a comparatively large degree of probability.

They represent well-defined targets and are detailed to such an extent as to be able to be translated into immediate action. Sometimes such plans are called projects, but in our opinion this term is more suitable for parts of a perspective plan.

The aims of operational plans are also limited in time. They have proved not to be operational if shorter than three months, which is the minimum limit for operational plans for the national economy of the U.S.S.R. and of East European socialist countries. This is being criticized and the minimum duration of a national operational plan is required to be one year.

It is interesting to note that operational managers (e.g., in Hungary) consider perspective plans too remote to have any practical meaning. They are not much concerned with the yearly plans either, their interest being centered on trimestrial plans for the fulfillment of which they gain personal rewards.[20]

---

are: (1) elimination of the existent difference in the conditions of production and life in the South and the other parts of the country; (2) an increased improvement of the agricultural sector and the conditions of life and labor of the agricultural population to render it comparable to the other sectors of production; (3) an appropriate urban settlement and a revision in rural building programs in order to create better living conditions for individual and social life, and to eliminate overcrowding; (4) implementation of a system of social security, hospital, and preventive medical services as required by a modern society; (5) formulation of a program adequate to new exigencies in diffusion of all instruments of knowledge and in particular education, scientific progress, and cultural and vocational formation.

The British plan has two overriding objectives: the increased economic growth and the solution of the balance of payments problems. This is meant to be achieved mainly through increased output, productivity and demand for labor on the production side, and on the requirements side by better use of resources in consumers' expenditure, social, public and other consumption.

[20] For the significance of trimestrial plans when managerial rewards are linked to them, see J. Kornai, *Overcentralization in Economic Administration*, translation from Hungarian (Oxford, Univ. Press, 1959).

C. THE CHOICE OF AIMS

The question is put forward: How many planning targets ought to be set? Is there a connection between the planning targets and the optimality of their number? These questions can be approached at three different levels:

(a) As to the number of indicators in one plan.
(b) The number of variants of one plan presented, i.e., should there be one or two, or several, or many variants of one and the same plan.
(c) The possibility of changing the planning aims.

In centralized Soviet planning there were at one time 19,000 groups of articles centrally planned and allocated. The figure mentioned at present is that of 14,000 groups. In Yugoslavia in the period of administrative planning there were 16,000 groups of such centrally planned articles.[21] In the new planning system introduced after 1952, there are no more than a couple of hundred such articles. The number of centrally planned articles is thus in the process of being greatly reduced. The same applies to planning in Poland, Czechoslovakia, Hungary, and East Germany.

Detailed planning means not only administrative allocation with all its shortcomings, but also less freedom of choice by the enterprises in the process of production and distribution of goods and consequently less choice for the consumer. Thus the reduction has meant also a greater freedom of action for enterprises and a decentralized system of economic administration.[22]

Both the French and the Netherlands plans have only macro-economic indicators whose number is rather small. In their case the main problem is how to reconcile the macro-planning targets with the micro-economic action of the firm, the latter operating through the planning mechanism of the firm on the market or through the market mechanism only.

In Soviet planning there was in principle no variant of State plans possible, as plans were authoritarian orders set by the central authority

[21] In the period of decentralization in the early 1960-ties the government of the USSR confirmed annually some 150 material balances. In the State planning commissions of the Soviet republics 1,600 balances were worked out, and the organs of material technical supply allocated the products on the basis of their 10,500 balances. V. S. Nemtchinov, *Ekonomiko-matematicheskie metodi i modeli*, p. 59.

[22] "The increasing centralization of the indicators system came to contradiction with the new conditions of development of the national economy, as it made the maneuverability of the resources more difficult in the course of the fulfillment of the plans and limited the operational autonomy of the organs of direct implementation of the plans." Kolodny, Stepanov, *op. cit.*, p. 40.

of the State. This rigidity caused many difficulties and therefore a procedure was developed to alter the plans after a certain time, in order to make them more realistic (the *rebalancing* of the plans).

In other countries more flexible approaches are found. The main request for the multiplicity of targets came from the political bodies, who complained that plans presented in one variant only put them in a position of having to accept them almost without alteration and that therefore the planners dictated the plans to the political bodies, thus causing tension between the planocrats and the politocrats to develop.

The French planners presented to the political bodies one plan only, but are considering working out several variants, which a formalized planning model would enable them to do more effectively. Moreover, opinions were expressed that the number of variants of a plan should go up to a dozen in order to make the planning aims more democratic.

On the other hand, the Swedish chief planner, I. Svennilson, considers that the presentation of more than one variant plays a somewhat demobilizing role by presenting too many alternatives and thus weakens the stimulative effect of the targets set. Therefore only one single variant should be worked out.[23]

D. DEGREE OF COMPULSION OF PLANNING AIMS

The degree of compulsion of planning aims should be discussed also, this problem being linked to the problem of planning discipline. How compulsory the fulfillment of planning aims is, depends on the planibility. The more planible, the less compulsory the plans should be.[24]

[23] P. Massé at the Second International Congress of Economists, Vienna 1962; Svennilson etc., Long Term Planning in Sweden, *Skandinaviska Banken*, No. 3 (1962).

In 1965 the French Government submitted to the Parliament only one project of the Fifth Plan, "with the aim to explain better the reasons which led the Government to stand for this orientation and to eliminate other orientations in order to make the debate clearer and more objective".

[24] In planning theory Soviet economists emphasize the distinction between the law of planning as an objective economic law and institutionalized normative law ("juridical laws"). Expression of such objective laws is found in the institutionalized state plans. In the new theory there is a warning against Stalinist voluntarism in planning, against departing from material conditions of development of the society and turning the plan into a game of figures. On the other hand, a warning is expressed also against the fetishization of economic laws, which denies the possibility of a conscious fulfillment of such laws; economic plans are determined not only by economic but also by political and other factors. Kolodny, Stepanov, *op. cit.*, p. 17.

As to the form in which planning aims can be presented, the main ones are the following:

(a) As a forecasting report of a government agency.
(b) A decision of a firm, etc.
(c) A contract between firms, bilateral or multilateral, or between firms and government agencies.
(d) A regulation or a decree of the government, a statement of a Minister.
(e) A law or a resolution of the legislative body.
(f) An international agreement.

Nevertheless the form does not always directly show the force of the planning aims concerning their fulfillment. In examining various plans we could establish the following gamut of degrees of planning discipline with regard to the fulfillment of the aims:

1. *Informative*

Informative aims are not more than *information* presented in a consistent form. Such aims let the economic actors who implement the plans know what useful knowledge of overall forecasts the plans can give them, but leaves it to them what to use and how to use it. Thus such plans could be called a one way generalized *information service.*

2. *Descriptive*

Here the aim of planning is to gather special information regarding other people's plans and to distribute it to all concerned, like a two way generalized *clearing house* of information or advertisement service. The planning aims may be just a juxtaposition of a mechanical sum total of individual plans or foreseeable decisions. Here again the role of the plans is passive, with no particular effort to achieve internal consistency, only coordination and avoidance of open clashes, letting those who implement the plans take the responsibility for how to make use of them.

3. *Indicative*

Indicative aims of plans. These are planning aims which give more than passive information, taking the responsibility of showing the objective which the planners consider should be the goal of the economic activity of those implementing the plans, in order to achieve micro-gains from macro-plans by their own action.[25] These might be compared to a generalized *market research* agency whose purpose is to act as a market catalyzer.

4. *Stimultative*

Stimultative planning is that in which the aim of the plan is to stimulate economic actors implementing the plan to action by giving them additional means out of public funds (collected from the community) as some sort of premium which will lead to the fulfillment of the planned aims. Thus this kind of planning also could be compared to a generalized risk-reducing mutual *insurance company*.[26]

5. *Competitive*

Competitive aims are those which are set by the plans, but the actors to whom the plan is addressed are left to compete as to which of them will

[25] The aim of the French plan was formulated as follows: to centralize and co-ordinate all information available regarding the variables which influence the economic future of the national economy, of each sector of activity, and as far as possible of each region. B. Cazes, *La Planification en France et le IVe Plan*, p. 10.

The indicative character of the French planning was particularly stressed in the Fifth Plan. "The Fifth Plan consists of a programmation of values. There is no question of objectives but of indication of conditions within which the evolution of principal economic magnitudes expressed in value can be compatible with the economic and social objectives of the nation." P. Massé, "Introducing the Fifth Plan", *Le Monde*, 31 July 1965.

The Japanese Five-Year Plan aims to provide "guidelines for economic activity to be conducted in a system of basically free enterprise and free markets." It endeavors to show the picture of the future Japanese economy as it should be, and provide criteria for the direction of private enterprise as well as government policy. It indicates the way in which basic industry should be developed, but does not aim to fix detailed targets in every sector since this would not be in conformity with the economic conditions of Japan. In many other places this character of the Japanese plan is underlined. It is said that it should provide guiding principles, to serve as signposts for private enterprises, and to give guidelines against which government economic policy will be decided. "Economic Planning Agency", *op. cit.*, pp. 6, 17.

[26] The relationship between the market and the plan is indicated in the British Plan as follows: "Most manufacturing industry and commerce is, and will continue to be largely governed by the market economy. But this does not necessarily and without active Government influence, bring about the results which the nation needs. ... Also the forces of competition often operate too slowly. ... Sometimes Government action may be required to strengthen the forces of competition. ... In other cases important social costs arise which are not expressed in market prices; and positive Government action is required to supplement market forces. ... Care will be taken not to destroy the complex mechanisms on which the market economy is based." *The National Plan*, pp. 2. 3.

fulfill the aims[27] or which means will be used to achieve the planned ends. These aims are substitutable with regard to actors implementing them.[28] Planning in this case can be likened to a generalized *stock exchange* of plans.

6. *Normative*

Normative aims are those which are set by the planning authority in the form of fixed norms, which cannot be questioned by those implementing the plans, but are also binding for those issuing them. Nevertheless the initiative is entirely with the superior planning organs, and those charged with implementing the plans are left with no decision of their own.[29] It is assumed that their own interests are best served when fulfilling such planning aims because the superior planners know what is necessary, or what is good, for the people. An analogy to this kind of planning could be found in a generalized *state budget*.

7. *Imperative*

Imperative aims are those which are set by the planning authority and have to be fulfilled by those implementing the plans with no initiative of their own nor any regard for their own gains or losses. From this angle we have to distinguish between:

(a) Where there is an obligation to fulfill the aims of plans but no sanctions are provided if they are not.

[27] There is criticism by some socialist authors of planning in non-socialist countries, based on the fact that no compulsion is provided for the setting of targets and the implementation of the plans. Therefore they express the opinion that plans cannot be fulfilled. This opinion is based on (a) their disbelief in the merits of forecasting and the influence of objective economic laws; and (b) their lack of understanding that targets can be set in such a way that private enterprises voluntarily collaborate to implement them. This is particularly the case where private concerns themselves influence or even lead the planning process.

[28] Both the British and the French plans, approved in 1965, underlined as one of the main objectives of the plan maintenance of international competition.

[29] The reform of the Soviet planning system in October 1965 stressed that the role of the State Central Planning Commission (*Gosplan*) USSR was to achieve unquestionable fulfillment of the State plan. The role of the planning commissions of the federal republics is to elaborate *projects* of the plans of the enterprises under the jurisdiction of the republics, and to make *propositions* to the State planning authority regarding projects of the plans of federal enterprises on their territory. Thus the role of the republics' planning authorities is only to make propositions and projects, but not to make decisions. *Law on the change of the system of organs of administration*, art. 7, Oct. 3, 1965. Cf. "Mazurov Report", *Pravda*, Oct. 3, 1965.

(b) Where there are material, moral, political, and legal sanctions if plans are not fulfilled, and rewards if they are.
(c) Where there is encouragement to overfulfill the aims in the plans, and, moreover, it is expected that the aims will be overfulfilled, this being the moral or political duty of all concerned.

The possibility of overfulfillment of the planning aims is not considered to be a case of bad planning and imperfect forecasting, but a virtue dependent on the special efforts and sacrifices of those who are economically active and are to be particularly rewarded without much regard for the fact that overfulfillment of the plans in one direction may cause shortage in another.[30] This type of planning can be considered as a generalized *command* or *war economy*.

8. *Punitive*

The aims of punitive planning are set with no regard to the interests of those implementing them; indeed they even may be against their personal interests. No gains are provided for those implementing the plans, which they have to fulfill under threat of punishment. Even the fulfillment of the plan is a punishment, as it is against their interests. This method of planning could be compared to a general *prison house supply system*.

[30] Only from 1959 the limits for certain target fulfillments were set. In order to prevent disproportions limitations of planned targets were introduced, and their overfulfillment prohibited. E.g. in 1959 there were limits of such kind set in 29 industrial branches for 734 products and in 1960 already in 36 branches for 896 products. *Kurs polititcheskoy ekonomii*, II, p. 497.

III. ACTORS IN PLANNING

The third element in planning consists of the persons (physical or legal) who act in planning. According to our definition of planning, it is essential that planning should be an institutionalized action. So the pertinent question to ask is who acts, for whom, and in whose interest.

This is also true for the comparison between planning in the East and in the West. We should dismiss the erroneous idea that planning in the East is a centralized, authoritarian system of one-party monolithic rule, while in the West there is a democratic system of free enterprise. This is an exaggerated oversimplification. Things are more complicated than that. In this section we shall discuss the actors according to their function in planning.

In every planning action there may be said to be four different functions and correspondingly four kinds of actors or organs of planning: [1]

(1) preparation of the plan
(2) decision making in planning
(3) execution of plans
(4) control of planning activity

There can be no planning without adequate actors specifically there to plan. One cannot plan with a liberal, "nightwatchman" government machinery.[2]

[1] The Egyptian planner, Abdel Rahman, called a similar set of functions a planning cycle. Dealing with the set of organs of planning, and being here more interested in the institutional side of the matter, we have given a combination of all four kinds of organs the name, planning center. I. H. Abdel Rahman, *The Requirements for Regional and National Planning*, Meeting of the Operations Research Society of America (Washington 1962), mim.

[2] Assuming that the structure of the planning mechanism is given, we could ask for help in determining the four functions in the process of planning from the management science:

Preparation of plans: Theory of need determination; assessment of wants and needs, means and ends, and turning them into planning resources and planning

A. PREPARATION OF THE PLAN

The organs of planning engaged in the preparation of the plan are those which perform the technical work through the following main activities: analysis of the results of the previous planning period; translation of political directives into actual planning targets; making changes in existing plans and preparation of new plans, balancing the planned requirements with planned resources.

To do this the actors are differentially organized: there are planning commissions, planning boards, planning institutes, planning commissariats, ministries of planning or of coordination, etc. In many countries there is a special supreme planning board, a collegiate body whose head is the head of the state or the prime minister, or a special minister of state, and which consists of a number of top government officials or political personalities, who accept the plan or give their final approval to the project of the plan, to be submitted to the legislative body. In principle the supreme planning board does not deal with technical problems; its main function is to reconcile conflicting views and interests of political bodies and of government departments. In many countries this coordinating function is reserved to the government, in socialist countries to the cabinet of ministers or to a special ministerial committee for planning.[3]

The organ for the preparation of the plan consists mainly of economists and technical experts, who prepare the projects of the plans from the technical point of view. The largest planning agency is that of the U.S.S.R., which has a staff that runs into thousands. Moreover, there is a

---

requirements. Model building in planning by choosing the determinants, the equations, the sets and exploring the values that make the plan consistent. Theory of data processing and collecting.

Decision: Theory of choice, fixing objectives and instruments, assigning the actors their role, selecting alternatives, evaluating them, and deciding on a solution.

Implementation of plans. Theory of persuasion – how to make the executants of the plans act and implement the plans; mobilizing actors in participation, getting approval for implementation. Theory of communication; formulating, splitting, addressing targets to actors; concretization and detailization of the plans; application of the specific language of communication in planning.

Control: Theory of testing; measuring aims against deeds; resources and requirements in plans against the attainment of targets; procedure and evaluation of testing, communicating results; closing the cycle of information by building controlled results into new plans. Cf., among others, P. P. Le Breton, *Planning Theory* (New York, Prentice Hall, 1961).

[3] For a comparative list of organization of planning agencies, see I. Tinbergen, *Central Planning* (Yale Univ. Press, 1964), Appendix, pp. 104-142.

similar organization in every Soviet republic, and in smaller administrative bodies. Organs of planning of like pattern are set up in every Eastern European country. The least institutionalized planning is that of Sweden, consisting of one Royal Commission appointed ad hoc for each plan, and a small permanent secretariat of up to three people in the Ministry of the Budget; most of the work is done by regular Government Departments, business organizations, and academic institutes.

The French Commissariat General du Plan has a staff of some 100 people and some 3,000 members of the modernization commissions. The Indian All Union Planning Commission consists of a large number of employees, which is no wonder for such a large country.

Symptomatic is the development in Yugoslavia. The Federal Planning Commission, when planning was on the administrative socialism centralized pattern, consisted of more than 1,000 people, and each of the six republics had several hundred. When a new economic system was established after 1952, the Federal Institution of Economic Planning consisted of only a couple of hundred people.

There is a constant danger that enlarging the staff of the planning agencies will lead to duplication of departmental administration, which creates tension and prevents regular administration from normal functioning.

The importance of the planning organ is often indicated by who is the head of the Planning Board. In the Eastern European socialist states he is most often a vice-president of the government. In other countries there is a special minister of planning, a member of the cabinet, who is the political head, and there is an administrative head under him on the expert level. In some cases the administrative chief of the plan is a public person of high standing, able to gain direct access to the head of the state and the prime minister. In other cases he is a senior government official, and the preparatory planning organ is a special agency attached to the prime minister's office or to the head of the state. It is considered to be either some sort of an economic general staff or an economic secretariat of top political officials. In some other countries there is a department in the Treasury (Ministry of Finance) which prepares the plans, having a senior civil servant as its head.[4]

It is the task of this body also to organize consultations with experts

[4] Planning in former British colonies in Africa is mainly of the Treasury type, while in former French colonies the planning agency is attached to the Prime Minister's offices.

and representatives of business organizations, of public administration, and academic experts.[5]

Problems arise in many countries as to the relationship between the proper planning function and operational activities.[6] In some countries the planning agency is an authority issuing orders and exercising administrative functions. In others this is not the case, the planning agency

[5] The French plan is a system in which the representatives of the State ... and the enterprises meet in an organized way to exchange information, to compare their blueprints for the future, and to act jointly in taking decisions and in forming opinions on the intentions of the Governments. F. Bloch-Laimé, *A la recherche d'une économie concertée* (Paris, 1959).

The British National Plan "was prepared by the Government in cooperation with private and nationalized industries, including representatives of management and trade unions. The National Economic Development Council was closely associated with the work throughout". The main body through which the consultation of the industries with the planning authorities takes place in Britain is the National Economic Development Council with which 20 Economic Development Committees are connected as well as 10 regional Economic Planning Boards and Councils. The Economic Development Committees consist of representatives of the management and the workers' unions within the industrial group, the representatives of the National Economic Development Office, and of the Government department sponsoring this particular industrial group, and also of independent members possessing expert and professional knowledge. *The National Plan*, p. A2, 44-45.

[6] Since most of the economic ministries were abolished in the USSR in 1957, part of their operational function has been transferred to the planning commissions. This, along with more general reasons, has led to a constant tension between the operational administrative agencies, the Economic Councils and the planning agencies.

In October 1965, decentralization along territorial lines was abolished, economic administration by ministries was reintroduced, and centralized planning was strengthened again. The reasons given for this change were the following: The territorial economic councils (*Sovnarkhozes*) were successful only in integrating small enterprises, in their specialization and cooperation, and in formation of repair shops. Their main fault was the slowing down of economic growth; the lowering of the quality of production; the disaggregation of branches of production which prevented them from being treated as one productive technical complex. The introduction of the Republic and federal Economic Councils and of the State Committees of the Soviet Government have not improved this territorial system of organization.

A multiple and cumbersome system of administration in planning was created. Before final decision was made, agreement had to be reached with the Economic Council of the region and the republic, the Republic Planning Commission, the corresponding State committee; the Committee for Scientific and Technical Coordination had to be consulted, and approval of the Soviet Supreme Economic Council and of the State Planning Committee sought. "Mazurov Report", *Pravda*, Oct. 3, 1965. In our opinion the mishap of the system of territorially decentralized planning in the USSR was due more to the battle between the half-hearted attempt at decentralization and the resistance of centralistic state bureaucracy which put obstacles to every attempt at independent decision, outside its own circles.

reserving its activity chiefly to preparation of the plans, their revision, research, etc.

Another problem is that of planning activity as competition between long-term and short-term planning. In the U.S.S.R. there have been constant changes over years in this respect. The federal planning agency was split into two, reunited again, and reformed after a period of time. In fact it is very difficult to separate long- and medium- from short-term planning. On the other hand, those planners engaged in day-to-day planning operations are inclined to neglect the study and research necessary for opening new avenues in long-term perspective plans.

B. ORGANS FOR DECISION MAKING

The final decision on which plan to adopt consists of a choice of alternatives and is made by a special set of organs.

In some countries the plans are finally approved by a special organ, a Supreme Planning Board. In others the plans are decided by the legislative body; this is particularly true for perspective plans, while yearly or shorter plans are decided by the government. Such a practice exists in Soviet-type countries, while in Yugoslavia both kinds of plans have to be approved by the legislative bodies. There are also countries where the plans are not decided by supreme political bodies but on a lower level, by such as ministers of finance, of planning, of coordination, etc.

A still more elaborate procedure was introduced in France in the 1960's: in 1964, Parliament passed a law on the options of the Fifth Plan on the basis of which the plan was prepared. Then, again, the project of the Plan, before being submitted to the Parliament, had to be discussed by the Economic and Social Council, and finally approved by the Parliament in the form of a law.

The decision of parliament can take the form of a law or of a resolution or some other form of parliamentary decision.[7] If the plan takes the form of a law it represents a special kind of law, which has only partly the binding force of a law. As the plan consists of forecasts with a greater or lesser degree of probability, there has been reluctance in recent years to give it the form of a law. In some parts of the plan the language also is

[7] On the legal character of plans in non-socialist countries, see G. Pescatore, *L'Intervento straordinario nel Mezzogiorno d'Italia* (Milano, 1962), p. 23, ss, 51, ss; For the Soviet type of planning, cf. P. Stajnov, Professor of the University of Sofia, "La nature juridique des actes de planification dans l'Etat socialiste" *Revue du Droit Public et de la Science Politique* (Paris, Sept.-Oct. 1963).

different from legal norms or legal rules calling for sanctions. Therefore there is a tendency to separate the normative part, containing the normative content of plans, from its analytical and forecasting content. The legal part consists mainly of definitions of economic instruments (taxes, rates of interest, etc.). In some instances there is a complete separation of the normative from the analytical part of the plan and from forecasting planning targets. The former is passed in the form of a resolution of parliament and the latter in the form of a law (e.g., the Yugoslav plan, 1964).

One has to distinguish the more stable economic instruments, which are a constitutive part of the economic system, from instruments related to the performance of the immediate fulfillment of the plan. The first can easily be separated from the text of the plan, which in this case will cease to be an omnibus law, while the others cannot possibly be separated from the final document on planning except formally.

C. THE ORGANS OF THE EXECUTION OF THE PLAN

The organs which take care of the execution of the plans are: different governments on central, regional, and local levels, or special government agencies and services, such as statistical offices, public bodies, and chambers of commerce. Other executants of the plans are business organizations: firms, factories, companies, corporations, banks, cooperatives, trade unions, etc.[8]

[8] The responsibility for the implementation of the plan is particularly stressed in the British Plan. "The plan is a guide to action. It must show who is responsible for what." For that purpose a very useful device, a "checklist" is inserted in the Plan, stating 33 major fields of action and for each of them, who is responsible for the implementation of the Plan. These 33 fields are grouped into five major groups such as: balance of payments, industrial efficiency, manpower, regional development, and public spending. In some of the fields the Government is solely responsible; in others the responsibility is shared with the National Economic Development Council and the Economic Development Committees, with other public corporations, the management and trade unions, National Labour Council, National Board for Prices and Incomes, etc.

The British Government is "discussing with industry (which means management and trade unions) the measures needed to implement the plan. Leaders in the management and the trade unions have a special responsibility". But the Plan does not stop at that and widely enlarges the circle of responsibilities. "The achievements of these aims will depend on the involvement and the acceptance of responsibility by individuals at every level in industry." Under industry all branches of economic activity are meant, including agriculture. Cf. *The National Plan*, p. A2, 16.

The targets are expressed in such a way that the organ which has to fulfill the plan is explicitly mentioned in the plan. This kind of direct micro-planning action is called: the plan addressed to a specific organ. Most of the planning targets are not addressed to any actor but are stated in macro-economic terms. The definitional delimitation between macro-economic and micro-economic plans runs exactly on this line. When an organization has organs of action which can act when addressed by the plan to do so, we talk of micro-economic planning. Such is the planning of firms, households, government agencies, etc. If there are no organs of action, but we have to infer them from the behavior of a group of economic subjects who act as if there were a common organ of action, we talk of macro-economic planning. Such is, e.g., planning of different industries, of sectors, regions, social classes, states, etc.

The Yugoslav Social Plans are macro-plans in those sections which are based on forecast of economic activities or of sectors, and which set the parameters of action for individual enterprises. They are micro-economic when they decide that such and such an enterprise will carry out a specific task, e.g., land reclamation in the Danubian Plain, and get for that purpose, say, 100 milliard dinars. The French plan is almost entirely macro-economic, dealing with sectors and industries and regions. In it no individual enterprise is ever mentioned, and planning targets are not addressed to any of them. Most national economic plans are macro-micro plans mixed in different ways. The Soviet-type centralized, authoritarian plans were predominantly huge micro-plans. The growth of the Soviet economy made the system of micro-planning on the national level impossible, and macro-planning developed to a much larger extent at the expense of national micro-planning, which is increasingly left to decentralized authorities and to the enterprises themselves.[9]

[9] "With the development of socialist society and the increase of the proportions of production it became impossible to make centralized decisions about all problems of socialist construction; therefore the gravitation point of operative decisions was necessarily transferred to those on the spot."

"Individual branches of industries and the leading links became more independent, which enabled them to make use of their experience and local conditions and particularities, and to develop the initiative of the workers and to introduce them to the management of the national economy." Kolodny, Stepanov, *op. cit.*, p. 58.

The reform of the Soviet planning in 1965 reapportioned the tasks of the State planning authorities and of the enterprises. It was considered no longer necessary to run the enterprises by detailed planning by the State administration, as this limited their independence and initiative and decreased their responsibility in the improvement of the organization of production.

"From now on instead of detailed plans of many indicators only the main

In many cases the planning of the private sector is macro-economic providing focal points for the activity of enterprises. The planning of the public sector is more micro- than macro-economic as targets are set for particular government agencies. This micro-macro relationship is of utmost importance for planning. In centralized planning it is often assumed that the central macro-economic plan is a sum of micro-plans as all micro-plans are linked together by a central plan. This is not correct, as these plans have direct and indirect effects which the centralized plan does not take into account (such as secondary investment effects, multipliers, accelerators, etc.). There is also the opposite view, that the micro-plans are mere parts of a macro-plan. This again does not hold, as the organs making micro-plans have their own interests, develop their initiative, and act in their own way, thereby sometimes preventing or adding more or less to the macro-plan than this plan foresaw or had formally recognized.

Thus there is a gap between the macro- and micro-plans which is filled in different ways, e.g., by the action of the market mechanism (as in France and the Netherlands) or that of the firm (as in the U.S.S.R.). This gap is deliberately left in France for the enterprises to fill according to their own interests, while in the U.S.S.R. two ways are open. One is that of urging the enterprises to overfulfill their plans, without much concern as to where the resources will come from for this extra effort. The other is that of underground, informal activity "by the left hand", which is carried out without formal approval, not registered by the macro-plan.

The execution of the plan demands a special institutional set of organs. These are sometimes established as parts of the government departments or parts of business management. There are two main principles of organization. One is a functional principle by which in every department the superior is directly linked to the inferior planning body and limits its activity. In this way the whole planning action is vertically organized as one monocentric system. But it overplays the role of planning by sub-

tasks of the enterprise will be planned by the authorities: such as the volume of sales; the basic list of products; the wage fund; the volume of centralized investments; the sum of profits; the proportions of payments into the state budget; etc." Other indicators and activities will be planned by the enterprises themselves, among other things: the number of personnel, the productivity of labor and the cost of production; internal reserves; the ways to increase productivity and lower the costs of production is better known by the workers on the spot than by the state planners. They will also decide about the use of their fixed and working capital, and the investment above the centralized plan. *Pravda*, Oct. 3, 1965.

ordinating all other activities to it, e.g., supply, labor, market, finance, etc. All management is absorbed in planning only. Therefore this system was abandoned and another put in its place, that of unified command where each level of decision making has its own planning service which is only one part of the decision-making process. Here the service of planning is dissected according to the general organization, and made subject to overall decision making.

D. THE ORGANS OF CONTROL

Control is essential in planning. As the output of one plan is the input of another plan, it is necessary to have a much stronger control of economic activities than in the market economy. Control can be exercised by varied methods, the most important of which are:

(a) *Material Control* of how the plans are being carried out in the product dimension, mainly done by statistical offices.[10]

(b) *Administrative Control*, controlling the execution of the orders of higher administrative organs by lower bodies, conducted through the regular administrative line of communication.

(c) *Financial Control*, referring to monetary expenditures and linked to the government budget, the volume of credits, etc. This is done for regular government expenses in the usual way of classical budget control, although it becomes more complicated because of spending on business activities. Moreover the banks, especially the central national bank, have control of other financial operations in most cases, not only of the foreign currency regime.

The relationship of public administration to business and other organizations is a special problem. As the plan aims to achieve the most important national goals, it is given a high priority, and all other functioning of government and business machines is subordinated to it. Nevertheless certain limitations have to be put on the fulfillment of the plan. Among them is the control by the public administration over fulfillment of such plans as sanitary control (e.g., of food and beverages), market control, veterinary police, labor relations control, etc.

[10] The British plan emphasized forecasting as a useful control device. "If an industry falls below projection it will be valuable to discover why. In some cases no action by Government may be indicated. But in other cases it will serve as a useful warning signal for action by industry, by Government, or by both in co-operation." *The National Plan*, p. 3.

There is no perfect harmony in the work of the planning organs. On the contrary they are antagonistic to each other in their functions. A constant tension exists between the organs for the preparation of the plans and the decision-making organs which require changes in the proposed plans. Moreover, sometimes liaison between the two is broken and the decision makers make decisions without much regard for the planning agencies, which then have to cope with the problem of consistency. This is particularly so if the main role of the planning agency is defined as the removal of disproportions.

Tension also exists between the decision makers and those who have to fulfill the plans. The former are, as a rule, overambitious from the point of view of the latter. On the other hand, the latter always try to plan less in order to be able more easily to overfulfill the plans and be rewarded for this. There are quite subtle ways of doing so, which the Polish economist O. Lange has described as a specific law of socialist planning. It shows that if a reward is given for the fulfillment of plans, the business organizations will always tend to put their targets lower than what is possible in order to be able to overfulfill them more easily and get rewarded; but they will not fix them very much lower, for fear that the higher planning authorities will then increase the norms of their planning targets.

Tension occurs, too, between organs for the execution of the plans and the control organs, which is only too natural and exists in all controlling agencies that have to judge the work of others. Therefore there is the usual complaint on the part of the business organization of the formalities of control, their complications, bureaucratic methods, incompetence, etc.

On the other hand, the controlling organs have to cope with the problem of false reporting, of double plans (one for the higher ups and the other for internal operational use), problems of hiding unused capacities from the planning authorities in order to achieve extra production outside the plans for themselves, stockpiling raw materials and finished products for extra activities, etc.

IV. INSTRUMENTS OF PLANNING

We understand by planning instruments the qualitatively and quantitatively defined means by which it is intended that the actors will achieve the planned aims. In other words, these are the means by which planned resources are meant to match planned requirements. The equilibrium between resources and requirements is expressed by planning targets which in this sense represent the "price". The requirements represent the "demand" (use, input), and the resources the "supply" (provision, output) side.

The planning instruments and their effect depend to a great extent on the level of development and on the structure of an economy.[1] Not all instruments are suitable to achieve the same planned goals at all levels of development, in all societies. Planning instruments which produce favorable results in one plan may not be successful in another. Therefore one must be careful when copying planning instruments from one plan to another.[2] But it seems to me that very few econometric models

[1] B. Higgins has distinguished three different types of planning which are, in his concept, three different applications of one general method: planning in (a) developed countries, i.e., industrially developed countries, where the growth is balanced and regular, and the purpose of planning is to correct the market; (b) developing countries, where there is a necessity to do more than correct the market; here Higgins advises investments in the public sector and control of the private sector; development has to be directed and planning by sectors becomes important; (c) non-developed countries in stagnation or decay. In such countries development is a cumulative process where action by shock treatment is necessary. The most important aspects of planning are those leading to structural changes. In this case planning has to assume the form and methods of the war economy, and Marx and Veblen are more important than Marshall and Keynes. B. Higgins, *Economic Development*, 1959, pp. 629-687.

[2] It was absurd when, e.g., small Albania planned its economic development on the same pattern of instruments as the huge Soviet Union. But a similar demonstration effect is visible to a certain extent in other socialist countries and their plans. Not long ago Soviet economists expressed the opinion that only the USSR and the People's Republic of China are large enough to plan a complete economy, e.g., to pursue a more or less autarchic policy. V. P. Miroshnichenko, ed., *v evropeyskich stranach socializma* (Moscow, 1962).

of planning based on parameters of action, correlations and propensities take into account this elementary experience. It is not only relations that matter but above all the magnitude of absolute figures.

There are many ways of classifying planning instruments, but the main division is into:

(a) Administrative Planning Instruments.
(b) Economic Instruments.
(c) Neutral Instruments.

Administrative instruments are those based on the use of power by the authorities; the economic instruments provide the actors with material gains if they fulfill the plans. In plain words, these two instruments represent the stick and carrot methods. The third group is composed of neutral instruments which intend to make the planning technique operate effectively.

A. ADMINISTRATIVE PLANNING INSTRUMENTS

By administrative instruments are meant acts of public authorities which are carried out with the intention of influencing the implementation of the plans. In the negative sense these are those based on fear of physical force.[3]

Various reasons are given to justify the use of force in planning, such as reasons of state, pursuit of progress, ideology of political parties, economic growth for the prestige or the competitive power of the state, its "historical mission", etc.

The administrative instruments may take effect in the following ways:

(a) They may appear in the form of the application of the authority of the state in its *legal* form: the constitution, laws, rules, regulations, decrees, etc., which set the government apparatus in action.

[3] There is the famous dictum of Stalin's that the Soviet plans are not plans-prognoses but plans-directives which must be implemented. The French plan too claims not to be a simple indication of tendencies. It has the purpose to "free the timid from fear and to make the prudent think" (Massé), which is neutral with regard to the economic finality of public authority, but "modifies the manner in which the decisions are made". Thus it not only regulates the flow of spontaneous activities, but directs them to certain priorities, indicated by the plan. Portugal's authoritarian plan states that it is "a norm of discipline of the intervention of the state in the economic market, for conserving and strengthening it, for giving initiative and regulating the competition of industries". In all, it has "to combine the forces of the Government and the Nation", which in our opinion may mean different things to different people. Presidencia del Conselho, *Projecto de Plano de Fomento para 1959-1964* (Lisboa, 1958), p. 5.

(b) There are *political* planning instruments which apply the pressure of political machinery, the push of party organizations, sanctions, lobbying, etc.

(c) Finally, there is economic pressure imposed by business organizations (monopolistic pressure) in order to set up the planning targets in their own interest.

In the Soviet planning system the main instruments of planning are administrative instruments, which have given to their planning system the name of administrative planning. These instruments reached their peak in the period of Stalin's Five-Year Plans. At that time there were no less than fourteen different kinds of planning disciplines imposed upon the actors in planning.

In Yugoslavia administrative instruments have been mainly replaced by economic ones, the main emphasis being laid on stimulating the material interest of those who have to fulfill the plans. There are safeguards for exceptional situations. When these stimulating instruments do not operate in a satisfactory way, the administrative instruments are called upon by the government to help until another economic instrument is put into operation.

The most frequently used administrative instruments of planning are these:

(1) *Foreign trade control and currency regulations are instituted.* In order to plan a country effectively it is thought necessary to establish some sort of filter or conversion points in which the international economic transactions are adjusted to the national planning mechanism. This is achieved by control of physical movements of goods, of prices, foreign and domestic, by control of the movement of current means of payment and of capital. The main purpose is to maximize the incoming mass of foreign currency. Another method is that of a profitable foreign trade, in which good care is taken not only of the balance of payments but of the prices and terms of trade. The first method can be tolerated when the foreign trade represents a small percentage of the national income and the state budget can cover the losses. But when international exchange grows beyond a certain quantity, this method becomes too costly and the second principle, that of planned profitable trade, has to be put into operation.

The degree to which instruments are used depends on various factors.[4] The main aim of such instruments in the Soviet-type planning is to

[4] In the globally-planned Soviet Union there is a state monopoly of foreign trade. In this way a system of domestic planning is created which operates under

keep the planned balance between imports and exports. The favorite method is that of bilateral clearing.[5] In underdeveloped countries planning of foreign trade has the main purpose of providing currency for imports of capital goods.

(2) *Tax policy* is an instrument of planning, very much in use in various forms.

The turnover tax is the instrument by which the demand for goods is meant to be reduced to the level of available supply. To achieve its purpose this instrument ought to be very flexible. It has turned into a major fiscal instrument of compulsory saving, and therefore has become very inflexible.[6]

Income tax as a planning instrument, besides its fiscal character, also has the purpose of reducing the consumption of goods with a higher coefficient of income elasticity or of transforming means of personal consumption into general government consumption through the State Budget.

Taxation is also used in other countries for stimulation of the fulfillment of plans.[7]

(3) The government, communal, and regional *budgets* are very

---

conditions that make the domestic economy not internationally comparable in cost, productivity of labor, etc., and the foreign exchange of goods takes place on a completely different basis.

In Yugoslavia the foreign-trade enterprises act on foreign markets, calculating their gains and losses independently. There is a plan for foreign trade which the enterprises set for themselves under guidance of the chamber of socialist business enterprises and its section of foreign trade, the Federal Secretariat of Foreign Trade, and the National Bank. Strict currency control with some small retention quotas acts as a stimulant for the enterprises engaged in foreign trade.

In India foreign trade restrictions were introduced particularly during the second Five-Year Plan, which put great strain on imports. It is assumed that in planning of developing countries there will be an increased pressure for imports and a reluctance to export. In this way two main trends in foreign trade development are noticeable, one aiming at achieving the maximization of the mass of foreign currency by forced exports below world market prices, and maximization of imports of capital goods at any price.

[5] Recently efforts have been made to introduce multilateral clearing and to liberalize the foreign trade in Soviet-type countries. For that purpose a joint international bank of the CMEA countries, was established in Moscow, in 1963.

[6] In Soviet-type planning this tax is the main source of investment funds. In Yugoslavia for this purpose a capital levy was established to which all enterprises had in principle to contribute yearly six per cent of their working capital. (From 1965, four per cent.)

[7] This is specially so in France where exemptions and special tax reductions are the most frequent instruments of inducement to private enterprises to act according to the national plans.

powerful instruments of planning by redistributing the national income.[8]

Sometimes there are complaints (e.g., in France) that the state budget is not concerted with the national plan. Different reasons are given such as the traditional way of financing government departments which are reluctant to accept the overall planning technique for reasons of conservatism, distrust of planners, demand for greater freedom of use of financial resources, and the jealously-kept authority of the Ministry of Finance.

(4) Aid, subsidies, and similar instruments of planning can have only a limited effect, mainly on income redistribution.

(5) Allocation of credits, particularly from public funds by administrative decisions, is another instrument of planning. This is particularly so with regard to investment credit policy. There are two different approaches. One is that investment ought to be allocated by administrative decisions which follow extra-economic aims of the plan with no regard to "calculations". If the funds are centralized such an investment policy ends in an income redistribution rewarding the unsuccessful enterprises at the expense of the successful ones. The other is that administrative decisions also have to take into account the profitableness of investments, and submit the extra-economic aims to evaluation by using economic criteria. Profitableness in planning has yet to be defined. In a centrally-planned economy it is not the individual gains of the enterprise that matter, but overall social gains. But there is not much agreement as to what social gains are and how they should be computed.

(6) Administrative fixing of planned prices is another instrument of planning.

(7) In the authoritarian type of socialist planning all wages are fixed by law, be they time or piece wages. Only a small amount is given in the form of stimulative wages and salaries from the manager's fund. In personal stimulation of the workers the main instruments are promotion in status, be it in the administrative hierarchy or in political organizations, leading to a rigid and inflexible ramification of such organizations.

[8] In Soviet-type planning some 66 per cent of the total national income is redistributed by the overall state budget, which is part of the state plan. This budget incorporates into one financial system the federal budget, the budgets of the Soviet republics, and those of local authorities, as well as social insurance funds, etc.

In other planning countries the budget is of less importance in planning, as between thirty to forty per cent of the national income is redistributed by the state budget. This is the case in Yugoslavia, in France, etc.

Promotion brings influence, power, and personal material gains of a kind not connected with the performance in planning.

(8) Other positive administrative instruments are public recognition for planning: medals of work, order of the hero of socialist labor, different awards; titles, such as champions of productivity, stakhanovites, novators, etc. Competitions are organized among different factories for the fulfillment of the plans, and flags, diplomas, and public praise are bestowed upon those who win. Such psychological means, although not to be underestimated, have a limited effect in the course of time, particularly if other conditions of work (e.g., real wages) are not satisfactory.

There are also negative administrative instruments based on punishment if the plans are not fulfilled.

Administrative planning instruments can also be divided into: regulative, operational, and organizational instruments.

(a) Most *regulative* instruments are those which decide about other people's behavior, permitting, forbidding or ordering certain planning activity of economic subjects. Such instruments are laws and regulations issued by the decision makers which have the force of law, of administrative acts, etc.

(b) The *operational* instruments deal with such planning actions as those which order the government planning agencies to take certain steps, and organizations and government enterprises to act economically in a certain way, to conclude business transactions, to organize production, etc.

(c) The *organizing* instruments are those which are used to direct other people's activity by creating institutional bodies and setting rules for their behavior.[9]

B. ECONOMIC INSTRUMENTS

Economic instruments of planning are such instruments as those which aim at achieving the implementation of the planned objectives by direct stimulation of the material interests of those actors who carry out the planning tasks. They operate under the assumption that these actors by

[9] The Soviet-type planning predominantly uses all three kinds of administrative instruments. If an order of priority had to be established, these would be put in the following order of importance: operational, organizing, regulative. In Yugoslavia the order of importance would be: organizing, regulative, operational. The French planning could be described as mainly regulative, to a certain extent organizational, and to the smallest degree operational. The Dutch planning uses organizing instruments to a small degree and operational and regulative instruments not at all. In Swedish planning almost no administrative instruments are used.

following their own specific interests (e.g., increase in personal income) will better fulfill the general aims expressed in the plan. For that purpose they must have a certain autonomy of will and freedom of action which will enable them to develop their initiative and energy in action.

The early puritan planners, thinking in terms of scarcity, considered it almost a sin to stimulate the direct producers by material gains. This was so until it became evident that economic growth imperatively imposes the problem of distribution of the goods produced,[10] and of further progress by creating new wants.

In Soviet planning very limited resources were allocated to personal stimulation of producers. On the enterprise level the only instrument of free material stimulation was the manager's fund, mainly, to give premiums and extra rewards to managers and top personnel. Also a very small share of the extra profits above planned profits was given to the enterprises themselves for small investments. Recently as the insufficiency of the administrative instruments became manifest, much thought has been given to economic stimulation.

The trend in this direction is as follows: [11]

(a) Individualization and liberalization of the enterprises, e.g., their change into "firms" which produce and sell their products under their own material responsibility, having their own trade mark.

(b) Products to be sold at market prices on the market according to the "law of value", and not under administratively planned prices.

(c) Payment of workers according to results, and gradual introduction of a kind of workers' management.

(d) Search for more economically motivated investment criteria.

(e) Decentralization of economic administration and of planning agencies, and abolition of the administrative role of ministries.[12]

[10] For changes in the system of planning in socialist countries, see R. Bićanić, "Economic growth, development and planning in socialist countries", E. Nelson, ed., *Economic Growth* (Univ. of Texas Press, 1960).

[11] For a description of new methods of planning being discussed in the USSR now, see UN-ECE, *Economic Survey of Europe in 1962*. Part I, pp. 45-50; Cf. also A. Nove, "Prospects for Economic Growth in the USSR", *American Economic Review*, May 1963, pp. 541-554; In Russian compare particularly B. L. Gontcharenko, ed., *Nepreryvnost v planirovanii i pokazateli gosudarstvenogo plana* [Continuity in Planning and the Indicators of the State Plan] (Moscow, 1962), a collection of 34 articles, among them one by Professor Lyberman, advocating the principle of profitableness in production. See also the Report of Mr. Khrushchev to the Central Committee of the CPUSSR, Nov. 19, 1962.

[12] The effects of centralized and decentralized planning are discussed in my article, "Economic Growth under Centralized and Decentralized Plannings", *Economic Development and Cultural Change*, No. 1 (Chicago, 1957).

In Yugoslavia economic instruments replaced administrative instruments in planning as early as the fifties.

The enterprises became independent and acted on the market, selling their products at the market price, achieving gains and suffering losses on their own responsibility.

Workers' management replaced the administrative bureaucracy in running the business enterprises, which decided autonomously about their plans.

Consumer credits are another instrument of planning, especially where consumer durables are concerned. Planning of consumer credits was considered in Soviet planning to be alien to a socialist economy, but when the production of consumer durables expanded it was successfully introduced.

The investment credits are allocated according to social plans on the macro-economic level, but distributed by the investment banks according to the rate of interest offered by the competing socialist enterprises on the micro-level.

The system of wages was altogether abolished, and instead a system of distribution of the income of the enterprises was introduced by which the workers' councils decide what part of the income, after taxes and social contributions are made, will be allocated by the enterprise funds and what will be distributed among the workers as their personal income. The workers gain their personal income according to their work, as measured by a system of points decided upon by the workers' council and depending on the productivity of the work on the personal level, the workshop level, and the enterprise level.

The principle "to each according to his work" is not limited to enterprises but is extended into communal planning and regional planning and leads to polycentric planning. Special care is reserved for underdeveloped areas, but the system is still one of their own participation in efforts and sacrifices.

In non-socialist countries the use of economic incentives in planning is apparently less developed. In some such countries there are beginnings of workers' management linked to planning.

In the Netherlands frozen wages enabled careful planning, until the shortage of labor spread "black wages". In France the trade unions were not interested in planning until recently, considering it a domain of capitalist monopolies.[13] But now the problems of income distribution and

[13] For the attitude of the Trade Unions in France to planning cf. Julien Ensemble, *Le contre-plan*, pp. 15-66. Paris, Seuil, 1965; The Swedish Trade Unions

of wage policy have again entered the sphere of economic planning.

In non-socialist countries, however, the main stimulant of enterprises is external. Enterprises are stimulated to fulfill plans largely by the following economic instruments: (a) information regarding business and investment prospects, and the government's domestic and international economic policies; (b) tax reduction if their activity is adjusted to plans; (c) government contracts; (d) subsidies and aid; (e) price policy; (f) granting of special credits for investment according to plan; (g) direct government interest in nationalized enterprises; (h) activities of government boards in bulk purchases and marketing.

The third group of instruments for planning are those which are neutral in that they use neither fear nor material gains as stimulants to implement the plans. Nevertheless they are necessary tools in the planning mechanism.

As a matter of principle the planning mechanism is supposed to make the economy transparent, and therefore information has to be carried on reciprocally from those carrying out economic activities to the planners, and from the latter to those charged with implementing the plans.

The following are the most important such instruments:

C. NEUTRAL INSTRUMENTS

(a) Recording of economic data relevant for planning. Collecting and processing of statistical data is a condition *sine qua non* for planning.

(b) Uniform accounting, which is an important instrument in planning. Such accounting was first introduced in Germany (E. Schmallenbach), and in the Soviet planning mechanism was adopted for the needs of a planned economy (Khozraschot). Such bookkeeping is of great technical help to any planning, as all enterprises are obliged to have uniform accounts.

(c) The obligation for all socialist enterprises to have their accounts with a socialist bank. This makes their financial operations transparent and controllable. Connected with this is a special organized service of social accounting, also an important instrument of control.

---

expressed their attitude to planning in *Economic expansion and structural change*, a Trade Union Manifesto, Ed. T. L. Johnston (London, Allen and Unwin, 1963), pp. 22, 28, 51, 164-168.

(d) The rule that in socialist planning all monetary transactions, with a few exceptions (payment of wages, retail trade; transactions of private households), have to be carried out through the National Bank. This was extended for a certain time to movement of goods, automatically followed by the flow of money in the opposite direction. The National Bank paid all bills without orders from the bearers of the accounts. Later this was changed in some countries when it was discovered that the flow of money does not neutrally follow the flow of goods but that there are special economic laws which govern it. Still, money is most planible, as it is the most abstract, homogeneous and common denominator in economic operations.

(e) Norms, both technical and economic.[14] These provide much help in calculation of costs and prices and in comparing them for planning purposes.

(f) The fifth French Plan introduced a specific kind of neutral instruments in order to keep the dynamic balance between the inflationary tension and the excessive slowing down of the economy. They represent signals for action of the planning authorities, when a certain line of deviation is crossed, or a limit of growth rate is not attained or is overstepped. These indicators are significant of the methods of open planning and give a predetermined and objective measure when the revision of the plan must be taken into consideration.[15]

(g) *Planning methodology*. It is considered that the method of planning is neutral and purely technical. Nevertheless it has an important bearing on the material side of planning and cannot be taken as technical. Formalized econometric models of planning also fall into this group of

[14] There are some 90 million norms in the Soviet economy, and standards of products embrace some 8,000 groups of articles; there is a uniform nomenclature for defining the products.

[15] These macro-economic indicators, called indicators of alert or flicker indicators are five, divided into two groups. The first group consists of two indicators: (1) The price level indicator, showing the rhythm of the annual increase of the consumer's price. If these prices increase by one per cent higher than those in the countries of the French commercial partners, action is required. (2) The Balance of payment indicators. This consists of the rate of balancing imports by exports computed by moving averages of 12 months. Red light is shown when the rate falls below the 90 per cent limit. The three indicators of the slowing down of economic life are: (1) The Growth rate of the gross domestic product. If the rate of growth is less than or equal to 2 per cent p.a. as computed by the Commission of National Accounts, the alert is sounded. (2) Productive investment indicator shows red light if the limit of growth of 2.5 per cent p.a. is crossed. (3) Underemployment indicator sounds alert if the number of persons seeking employment reaches 2.5 per cent of the active population.

instruments. To plan is to seek a balance between resources and requirements over time, and economic models represent the technique of achieving this. Formalized planning models meet with resistance from several quarters. Some reject them altogether on the grounds of their lack of perfection, without trying to make better ones. Others consider them as an infringement of their freedom of action as the consistency of the models prevents voluntaristic action in planning. This increases the responsibility of the planners, particularly on the decision-making level in governments and in Parliaments. Nevertheless econometric models of planning are gaining ground.[16] This had led the leading Soviet economist of the quantitative analysis school, the late V. S. Nemtchinov, to define planning thus: [17]

"Practical planning consists in harmonious coordination of the economic principle of conscious control of the social production (in accordance with the known objective laws of economic development) with the cybernetic principle of the automatic, autoregulatory and auto-organizing flow of the economic process. It is not an easy but a perfectly feasible task. This solution is possible only under certain decentralization of the planning decision making, reserving the most important function, and decisions regarding the principles of planning, to the directive-issuing centers, and transferring a considerable mass of problems connected with economic planning to the leadership of local organs, which will make decisions about them following the principle of democratic centralism."

Practically at the same time, the leading French planner P. Massé discussed at the International Congress of Economists in Vienna in 1962 the merits of a formalized as opposed to the discretionary model in French planning, which would consist of a large number of decision centers in the game, the State being the privileged decision center. The model would consist of a set of technical variables, a set of political variables, and a number of exogenous variables, and "the political choice

[16] In European socialist countries efforts to plan by using a formalized model are gaining ground. There are discussions about the Polish, the Czechoslovak, the Hungarian, etc., models of planning; their official formalization and practical application are still to be desired.

[17] V. S. Nemtchinov, *Ekonomiko-matematicheskie metodi i modeli* [Economic-Mathematical Methods and Models] (Moscow, 1962), p. 52. In this book Nemtchinov still stood for directive-issuing centers and democratic centralism in planning, but he also emphasized the role of the objective laws in economics, the process of auto-organizing floes and functional and spatial decentralization.

For the Western counterpart on the same subject of models, see I. Tinbergen and H. C. Bos, *Mathematical Models of Economic Growth* (New York, 1962).

would lose its meaning if it were not to be exercised between technically optimized variants".[18]

The consistency of forecasts of production and demand in the British plan was achieved by using, on one side, the estimates of the demand made by various industries for their products which were compared with the estimates of the Department of Economic Affairs, derived from the macro-economic pattern[19] of growth of final consumption, investment, export demand, etc.

Both of these cases show that the instruments of methodology are not so technocratically neutral as some might think. They lead not only from centralized to decentralized planning in the spatial sense, but, what is much more important, from monocentric to polycentric planning in the functional sense, and this has wider economic and social, political and technological implications.

[18] P. Massé, *Discretionary or Formalized Planning* (International Congress of Economists, Vienna, 1962).

[19] The formalized model which was used for converting the final demand into a pattern of growth was that of the Social Accounting Matrix and models associated with it, which were developed by the Cambridge Department of Applied Economics (R. Stone). (*The National Plan*, p. 33.)

For the Cambridge model see *A Programme for Growth, I. A Computable model of Economic Growth; II. A Social Accounting Matrix for 1960; III. Input-Output Relationship 1954-1966.* Published for the Department of Applied Economics University of Cambridge by Chapman and Hall 1962-1963.

PART II

ON MONOCENTRIC AND POLYCENTRIC APPROACHES TO PLANNING

INTRODUCTION

Polycentric planning finds its place on the agenda today whenever there is discussion of how to solve certain difficulties in planning such as the following:

(1) There is an ever greater need for the modern enterprise to plan. It is compelled to it by technology and the development of the economy. Planning has regained importance on the national level as well. The problem now is how to reconcile the plans of the enterprises and social or national plans, i.e., how to integrate micro- and macro-planning.

(2) There is the problem of reconciling political democracy and economic planning. What is the function of the political and what of the planning organs, or, to narrow the field, how should the elected politicians and the technical, planning experts interact?

(3) In multi-national federal states, with several political centers, planning is faced with specific difficulties. There is also the question of how to plan on an international scale with several sovereign states involved.

(4) There are specific problems facing planning in developing countries, where important institutional and structural changes are taking place. These are of particular importance for planning in countries building socialism.

(5) The great advances in statistical methods, computing machines, and cybernetics make possible a planned approach to problems hitherto insoluble. They have an effect also on the complexity, magnitude, and speed of solving the problems by integrating decisions of many centers.

In order to contribute towards a solution of these problems we are trying to develop a theory of polycentric planning. Our intention is more to stimulate thinking than to present ready-made solutions which would need a much wider scope than the present paper.

I. THE PLANNING MECHANISM

Just any kind of decision on future socio-economic activity cannot be called planning. On the other hand, the concept of planning cannot be limited to the method of centralized and authoritarian decision making for the future.

A. DEFINITIONS OF PLANS

By the term planning we understand rationalized, *ex ante* quantified economic development, over definite periods of time, carried out by specifically institutionalized human activity in a certain area, and with the use of instruments chosen in advance, with the purpose of achieving socio-economic gain.

(1) It is *institutionalized* development, answering the question, "Who is planning with whom and for whom?", i.e., planning requires specific planning organs or agencies, which are essential in order for planned action to take place.

There are four kinds of such organs: (a) for the preparation of the plan, (b) for decision making concerning the plan, (c) for the execution of the plan, and (d) for its control.

The organs for the *preparation* are various planning commissions, institutes, boards, or agencies. The *decision* making organs are parliaments, governments, boards of directors, etc. The *execution* of the plan is carried out by ministries, directorates, local governments, managers of business enterprises, workers and employees, cooperatives and producers' organizations, etc. The organs for the *control* of plans are various planning control agencies, ministries of finance, national banks, statistical offices, national uniform bookkeeping departments, etc.

(2) A plan must be *quantified*, answering the question, "How much of what?" Without quantification of requirements and resources consist-

ency of the plan cannot be achieved, and consistency is the main quality of any plan.

(3) Planning is based on *forecasting*, i.e., on statistical laws and probability calculus, answering the question, "When, and probably how accurate?"

(4) Planning is *periodicized* action, i.e., it refers to a definite period of time. The time dimension shows when the planning action begins, when it ends, and how it changes with time.

(5) Planning is a *rational* process measuring gain and waste from planning, giving the answer to the question, "Does a certain planning activity pay or not?" In other words, the question, "For how much?" demands an answer.

(6) Planning makes use of *knowledge of economic laws*; it is neither a traditional, nor a voluntaristic, nor an empirical method, but a scientific rational method weighing reasons and counter-reasons in giving an answer to the question: "How?"

(7) Planning is action developed on a *definite* area which can be homogeneous or heterogeneous (one or several plans covering an area, i.e., a state, a region, etc.). A plan must give a definite answer to the question, "Where is the planning action taking place?"

(8) Planning is carried out by definite *instruments* applied in order to achieve a planned product. It also determines techniques and methodology in the working out of the plan. Planning must be a conscious human action, a *deliberate developmental* activity. Thus planning cannot be a spontaneous economic activity.

(9) Finally, planning implies action towards *fulfillment of aims*, and this must be measured by balancing the planning requirements with the planning resources. It would appear unnecessary to underline this, but the experience of planning has shown that the rational selection of planning targets is often overwhelmed by considerations of other nature (political, ideological, strategic, etc.).

We would consider as planning only complex socio-economic action which includes all the elements enumerated above. Other forms of economic policy action could be given different names such as policy, programme, project, etc. But the term planning we would reserve only for actions which have all the qualities specifically described above.

By a planned economy, then, we understand that type of national economy in which the planning mechanism dominates all other mechanisms in the economic process.

B. THE UPPER AND LOWER LIMITS OF PLANIBILITY

In order to compare the effectiveness of planning with other mechanisms we must have methods to measure its performance and show the gain and waste derived from planning. Under gain we understand the positive difference between the results of the operations of a planning mechanism and that which would occur if this mechanism did not operate at all. The negative difference we call waste. Here not only micro- but also macro-effects have to be taken into account. These are sometimes called parts of social gains or costs, and include as well effects of planning outside the economic interest (extra-economic planning) and the operational sphere of micro-subjects. This measurement is a very complex process, in which economists have not made great progress so far. The first step is to establish the limiting points of the operation of a mechanism.

As planning depends on the level of economic development we would call *planibility* the degree to which an economic process is objectively suitable for planning. Planibility is, e.g., greater in manufacturing industries than in agriculture, greater in livestock breeding than in crop growing, greater in internal than in foreign trade.

The degree of planibility determines the upper and lower points of net gains from planning. These are determined by technical and economic dimensions, that is according to whether we can plan – i.e., whether the technique of planning gives sufficiently effective instruments to influence the economic process (the technical dimension) – and whether it pays to do so (the economic dimension).

The *upper* limiting point of planibility is such that it would be economically useful to plan but technically it is not possible to do so because we do not have adequate instruments (e.g., planning of weather, foreign trade, etc.). The *lower* limit is that point at which planning is technically feasible but not economically justifiable.

We can say accordingly that the technical dimension shows which combination is technically feasible, i.e., the limits of the substitution of factors in planning. The economic dimension gives the answer to the question, "Which combination gives the optimal gain or the minimal waste?"

Another dimension should be brought in, the *political* dimension which shows at what point political responsibility has to be taken when extra-economic considerations in planning lead to decisions on other gain and waste than those the economic indicators show, i.e., when the political optimum is different from the economic one. The political actors who set such claims carry the political responsibility for them, but in order to gauge the importance and the risk of their decisions it is the duty of the planning expert to find out which is the technical, which the economic, and which the political optimum, and measure the difference between the gains and losses. The planner then has to present the outcome of his calculations to the political decision makers.

Between the two extreme points, lower and upper, is the zone of planible activity, i.e., where planning is technically feasible and economically gainful. In this zone is a point of optimum which can be attached to each of the dimensions, to the best combination of several, or to all of them (optimum optimorum). In this way we can talk of the optimization of a plan maximizing various variables and putting constraints from the personal point of view (optimal for whom), from the production side (optimum of what), the spatial (where), the temporal (how long, and when), the instrumental (with what), the technical (how), and the compensatory (for how much), as well as from the point of view of management (who is capable of implementing the plan best). The problem of optimization is linked to the study of the aims in planning.

C. CHOICE OF STRATEGIC DECISIONS IN PLANNING

A total plan in which all the decisions in the national economy could be foreseen, and targets, instruments and actors decided on, does not exist and never did, nor can it be supposed that it ever will in any society. The magnitude of endeavoring to achieve such a thing may be illustrated by the calculation made in the Soviet Union that a complete plan of production and consumption of coal in the U.S.S.R. would have to consist of two and a half million indicators. If a relatively homogeneous product such as coal requires so many elements it is not easy even to imagine how many would be necessary for a modern national economy where there are several million kinds of goods. In Soviet planning, until recently, material balances were made centrally for fifteen to nineteen thousand groups of articles. One has to bear in mind that today, in the U.S.S.R., four thousand sectors are considered and that of this number only five hundred are planned as strategically decisive. In the country where planning is most detailed, of several million kinds of articles produced, only several thousand or even several hundred products are planned centrally. Indeed of the very great number (millions) of decisions which have to be made in every economy there are only several hundreds or thousands which are of strategic importance for planning. Thus this question is not only one of a formal and methodological character, but of the substance of planning – how the selection of decisions is made, on what principles, and for what purposes a specific choice is made, with what aim, why, how much and where planning is taking place.

This opens up the question of the *transmission* of strategically important planning decisions to other activities. Other decisions may be dependent on such strategic decisions, or independent from them. They may also be residual, i.e., decisions which the plan does not influence or is disinterested in. A whole set of questions is related to the field of planning decisions and their fulfillment. Do the planning decisions affect the total economic process or are they limited to giving the lead? By what mechanisms are the planning decisions carried out, and by what mechanisms the non-planned decisions market, contract, command, or household? One should not forget that even in the most centralized, authoritarian planning the number of decisions not included in the plan is very large, being far more numerous than the planned decisions. Of these only a certain number are induced by the plan, others are autonomous.

D. PLANNING AS AN ECONOMIC NECESSITY

Planning is not necessary nor is it possible at all levels of economic development, but at a certain level it becomes of such importance that performance of the economy cannot be achieved at the optimum rate without it. In other words, there is a level of economic development where planning can better solve the problem of optimal economic growth than can other mechanisms – market, administrative, etc. A short enumeration of the causes that make planning a necessity is given here:

(1) *Technological causes.* (a) Great concentration of the factors of production, depending on their technological *indivisibility*, which cannot stand the risks of the market, and demands minimization of such risks; (b) quick technological changes which require accelerated adjustment of capital goods and depreciation of fixed capital to be carried out, not according to technologically fixed rates, but because of economic obsolescence; (c) slow, short-term changes of current product-mix – the switch from one product to another – require an ever greater time period, and during this period current production cannot stand the hazards of sudden, great and accidental fluctuations on the market; (d) the very great changes in technology *caused by research lead* to the

introduction of new products on the market which are not induced by changes in demand, but which must be promoted by the deliberate action of the producer; (e) the technique of mass production that requires larger and larger markets and goes beyond the boundaries of existing institutions, markets, and administrative set-ups. It also leads to the appearance of administered prices, which are not market-conforming prices.

(2) Among the *economic* factors necessitating planning the following should be stressed: (a) the necessity to control cyclical movements; (b) the split between ownership and management, so that the maximization of the profit of the owners no longer guides the operation of enterprises. (Capitalist shareholders do not carry the current risk, and the financing of the enterprise is alienated from the dividends; in a socialist economy social ownership is completely separate from the function of management, which is even the case when management is carried out by workers' councils.) (c) The macro-effects are distinct from the micro-effects, and their difference is the smaller the greater the integration of the economy, which happens only on higher levels of development; (d) there is an ever greater number of partial extra-economic aims for which economic efforts are required, such as: accelerated economic growth for reasons of competition between different social systems, or disarmament, rearmament, abolition of national dependence, or increase of political independence.

(3) The increasing progress of *economic knowledge*, perfected statistical methods, and computers make a better control of economic processes possible. In this way economic science plays a never more effective and operative role in economic policy and planning, so that these latter become more understandable and accessible to a greater number of people. It goes without saying that political conditions and socio-economic systems play an important role in economic planning.

E. PLANNING IN CAPITALIST, IN SOCIALIST, AND IN DEVELOPING COUNTRIES

(1) In capitalist countries planning is most practiced on the level of micro-planning, in big corporations and groups of business enterprises. It is thus limited by the size of the enterprises, and their economic interest. Within the sphere of interest of business enterprises, planning by contract (where elements of the planning and contract mechanisms are mixed) is gaining more and more ground.

On the other hand, in many capitalist countries macro-economic planning is developing more and more; it (a) consists in substituting for the market mechanism macro-planning on the part of the state and public agencies wherever private enterprises have not enough interest to operate, or, (b) has a character of administrative planning wherever it is necessary for reasons of state to replace the inefficiency of the market mechanism in order to assure the proper functioning of the economy; (c) the contract planning mechanism is often found in the sphere of co-operation between government agencies and private enterprise (national defense, scientific research, etc.).

(2) In socialist countries planning is more and more becoming the dominant mechanism. In some countries the influence of the administrative mechanism and of the central state agencies still prevails over the social planning mechanism and planning operates more as an etatistic imposition than as a social service. The market mechanism plays a subsidiary role, although there is continuous tension between the planned proportions and their disturbance by the market mechanism (which means that the market mechanism is sometimes stronger than the planning mechanism). The contract mechanism is expanding in the field of cooperation with the private sector in agriculture, in activities among socialist enterprises (if they are independent) and particularly in international planning by agreement between various countries.

Since the late fifties there has been a tendency in socialist countries towards greater liberalization from the grip of the administrative mechanism, and an increased mixture of elements of the market in the planning mechanism. It is shown in such features as: decrease in the influence of central planning; decentralization and regional planning; increased independence of the socialist enterprise; the greater importance given to initiative based on the self-interest of the producers themselves.

In almost the same period another tendency has appeared in the advanced capitalist countries, which have begun to make wider use of planning and to increasingly rely on the planning mechanism. Some people attribute this converging tendency, so to speak, in both systems to competition between them; others to pragmatism, trying to learn from each other. In our opinion both tendencies have as their underlying cause the great changes that are taking place in modern technology, changes which we have already mentioned, and which necessarily require an ever greater use of planning of the kind we have described as polycentric.

(3) In the developing countries the problem of planning is particular-

ly complex. For their development they do not necessarily require planning within the whole framework of the national economy, and most often this is not even possible. On the other hand, their relative penury and the disproportions in production factors imperatively put on the agenda of economic policy the optimal use of these factors. Accordingly there is partial planning in the narrow sense, i.e., such as planning operations of the administrative mechanism and its influence on other mechanisms (market, firm, etc.).

Countries in the process of development are often thought of as those where the only applicable method of planning is a system of central and authoritarian planning as strict as possible. In fact, as in most cases planning is limited to the concentration of financial resources in the state treasury, and to the centralized and authoritarian decision making on spending for investment of these resources. However, this is aggravated by partial character of planning which covers only one, small part of the socio-economic process – the monocentric planning of the activities of the central government. It is better for such activities to be planned than casual, and it would be difficult to apply methods of social planning for the solution of their problems of centralized administration. Social planning requires a certain level of economic development, as we have said before, and therefore is quite different from central administering. There is no doubt that concentration of resources is useful to build up the infra-structure in the country, but there are some dangers against which a warning is not out of place.[1]

[1] For instance, there have been cases where the accumulation of resources for a partial plan, and their concentration on that plan only, have led to the neglect of other activities which could produce better results. Thus when planning becomes a fetish it may have a demobilizing effect on economic development. In this case planning has been some sort of alibi for errors of economic policy in many other fields.

II. MORPHOLOGY OF PLANNING

So far we have compared planning to the market, as a one-plan-to-one-market relationship. The discussion of the relations between the plan and the market is almost as old as planning itself. Their relationship has usually been presented as the problem of replacement of a market by a plan. This approach seems to us to be open to three objections: (a) There is no question of interrelationship between *one* market and *one* plan but between a *market mechanism* consisting of a great number of different markets, and a *planning mechanism* composed of one, several, or many plans. In a concrete market economy we have always to deal with a mechanism consisting of a great number of markets of different form, size, and degree of imperfection. In a similar way it is necessary to take into account that a planning mechanism also can consist of a smaller or greater number of plans. (b) There are more than two mechanisms in the game. In a modern industrial society we can find at least five mechanisms – the household, the market, the mechanism of the firm, the administrative and the planning mechanisms, for instance. And in a changing traditional economy there are even more to add (the tribal, the village community, etc.). Therefore, planning is not a substitute for the market in the sense that it exhausts itself in performing economic functions *instead* of the market. Planning can perform some economic functions at a certain level of development which the market mechanism cannot perform, and it can also carry out some other functions better than the market mechanism can. This, of course, applies in the reverse, too: certain economic operations can be better (i.e., more economically) performed by the market than by the planning mechanism and this applies also to other mechanisms. The plans can be in different mutual relations and this is the subject of research on the morphology of planning. Moreover, in every concrete planned economy there are different relationships between the planning mechanism and the other mechanisms – market, administrative, household, and firm, competing or cooperating with each other.

A. MONOPLANS, OLIGOPLANS, AND POLYPLANS

From the point of view of the position and interaction of plans in a planning mechanism we propose to distinguish monoplans, oligoplans, and polyplans. These various plans are units of the planning system.

A *monoplan* exists when the planning mechanism is formed of one single plan which is decided upon and carried out autonomously, with no regard to any other plans. In this sense it is necessarily an authoritarian plan.

An *oligoplan* is a component of a planning mechanism consisting of several plans, each of which takes into account the other plans with which it is competing. This competition can be based on different dimensions of planning: personal (competition of different actors in decision making), product (competition or substitution of products), spatial (several plans operating in the same area), time (plans, overlapping in time), instrumental (struggling for the same means, e.g., investment funds), institutional (conflict of authority of different planning agencies), etc. In short, competition among plans can occur in many dimensions.

The oligoplans thus influence each other, and each must take into account the other plans within the planning mechanism, i.e., no one plan dominates the others, there is no "top plan" but several plans exist on a competitive footing, on an equal level of decision making. Nevertheless they form one and the same planning mechanism.

Polyplans are those in which the planning decisions are made, and the initiative carried out for each plan, independently,[1] but they are interconnected within the framework of one planning mechanism. No polyplan can by itself influence decisions in other plans within the same mechanism. Plans can only influence each other jointly (i.e., the planned input of one polyplan is not the planned output of another but the sum of all inputs of all plans equals the sum of all outputs of all plans. They jointly form a closed, consistent matrix).

This classification is obviously inspired by the theory of imperfect competition, which we consider not only useful, but also justified, as planning is an extension to the extreme of imperfect market mechanisms. In our research into planning mechanisms we were able to profit from theories of imperfect market competition. Nevertheless the similarities of terminology should not prevent us from seeing the basic differences between the market and the planning mechanisms.

[1] Otherwise they would just be part of another plan. The closest concrete example of a pure polycentric planning mechanism is a set of physical town plans in an urbanized area.

(1) A market always consists of two sides – the buyer's and the seller's – while in planning there is one side only – the planner's. The former has partners and competitors and the latter integrates the functions of partners and competitors within the planning agency.

It is essential for the existence of the market that the actual partner is not known in advance, while in planning it is essential that the partners be known. In principle the transparency of the plan is supposed to be perfect from the point of view of the personal dimension.

(3) In the market mechanism the results are known *ex post*, while in planning the results are considered *ex ante*.

(4) Equilibrium on the market is achieved at the level of market prices, which represent the meeting point of demand and supply. With planning the equilibrium is anticipated by the planning targets (the "price"), and the action of the fulfillment of the plan (parameters, proportions) is directed so that the planned resources meet the planned requirements at the point of the planned target.

These differences mark essential distinctions between planning and market mechanisms, and the analogy of the terminology should not deceive anyone.

B. MONOCENTRIC, OLIGOCENTRIC AND POLYCENTRIC PLANNING

Among various possible types of planning mechanisms we select only a few for special consideration – the monocentric, the oligocentric, and the polycentric mechanisms. This classification is based on the number and functions of the planning centers in a planning mechanism.

We take a planning center to be the place of contact of all four essential functions of planning – preparation of plans, decision making, execution, and control. A planning center is a complete set of all four organs necessary for planning action.

Monocentric planning mechanism is a mechanism which, in a pure form, consists of one planning center and one autonomous monoplan only.

In a mixed form the whole economic process is planned by one autonomous planning center only and all other plans are deduced from and subject to it.

By oligocentric planning mechanism we understand planning of the economic process whereby the planning mechanism consists of several planning centers making oligoplans, each of which centers has to take into account the others but none of which dominates the economic process nor the planning mechanism.

The polycentric planning mechanism is understood to consist of a great number of planning centers making polyplans, none of which dominates the others but all of which are subject to a relationship determined by their mutual interaction.

Monocentric and polycentric planning are based on two different models of planning showing opposite tendencies. Taking into consideration only two dimensions – the product and the compensation, i.e., using price elasticity of demand as an indicator – we can distinguish two types of planning. One operates when the price elasticity approaches zero. In this case we are dealing with a mechanism of perfect monopoly-monopsony which represents the most completely centralized economy, where the market mechanism no longer operates and the price changes its character. On the other hand, when the price elasticity of demand is infinitely great, the price mechanism does not operate here either, and must be replaced by other mechanisms as allocators of goods. In either case, the infinitely small or the infinitely great elasticity leads to other-than-market mechanisms to satisfy demand. Their infiniteness calls for deliberate human action instead of the "invisible hand" of the market mechanism. The first is the model on which monocentric planning is based. The second is the model for polycentric planning.

Mixed monocentric planning is a heterogeneous planning mechanism whereby all plans are concentrated under one autonomous central one, which directs not only the movement of capital and products, but also of human beings. The volume of production is perfectly inelastic, determined by the central planner. Prices are voluntaristic, separated from costs in order to maximize saving and investment. The total gross national product is redistributed by the central plan on the macro-economic and the micro-economic level. Thus economic growth can be maximized at any cost by the autonomous decisions of the central planners, and the investment funds are accumulated in such a way that the consumption fund remains residual. The producers' income is determined by other criteria, i.e., administratively allocated priority or anticipated interest on capital, but not by the effect of work or efficiency. Thus there is an inflationary element built into the planning model. Foreign trade is dominated by the tendency towards autarchy, and the whole system necessarily tends towards bureaucratic or technocratic management from one center which knows no competition and allows for no alternatives. In practical planning the monocentric mechanism is identified with centralistic and authoritarian planning and is often presented as the only possible system of planning.[2] In our opinion the assumption: centralization equals rationalization equals optimalization has to be put to question in planning as well as in other fields of human activity.

C. CENTRAL PLAN AND MONOCENTRIC PLANNING

Differences must be emphasized between the central plan and the monocentric plan. A monocentric plan is a theoretically pure type of plan, while a central plan is a conglomerate document of concrete economic policy consisting of non-homogeneous parts. This non-homogeneity of the central plan is expressed in almost all planning dimensions, although it is often mistakenly assumed that a central plan is homogeneous and monolithic.

If we analyze central plans we will find in most of them the following elements: (a) one macro-economic model of planning economic growth (be it an empirical, discretionary, or formalized model); (b) a number of micro-economic regulative decisions of the central administration prescribing the behaviour of administrative agencies and of economic enterprises of different sectors; (c) organizational measures which include organization of the planning mechanism and its relationship to the market, the contract, and the command mechanisms; (d) operational decisions at the macro-to-micro level for accumulation and distribution of financial resources by the central government; (e) micro-economic plans of central government agencies; (f) micro-economic decisions for a number of particular concrete projects.

The heterogeneity of the central plan, on different levels of planibility, leads to different criteria for the consistency of the plan. If all these varied elements of the central plan are included in one document, their character and their function are no longer clear. The organs of planning, instead of performing a public service, then become the annex of the central politocracy or bureaucracy, which looks at the whole planning process through the eyes of its specific interests or, at least, preferences. Instead of scientific methods of planning a bureaucratic or political voluntarism appears, and instead of rational allocation of planned re-

[2] It has become customary, but wrong, from our point of view, to call all planned economies centrally planned economies. The adjective "centrally" obviously implies that there are some non-centrally planned but nevertheless planned economies. Also quite a number of people wrongly think a monocentric mechanism most efficient and most rational, indeed the optimal method of national planning.

sources operating by the strength of their rationality an authoritarian command of planned proportions comes into being, imposed by the power of the central government on both producers and consumers.

The heterogeneity and complexity of central planning, as well as the different degrees of planibility, are also derived from different levels of economic development, from differences in macro- and micro-economic planning, from different class structures of society, from different political systems, etc. Therefore it is quite in order in connection with centralized planning to ask the questions, "What do we centralize when we centralize?" "Do we centralize the preparation of the plan, the making of the decisions, the physical and the financial means for their fulfillment, the operators who have to carry them out, or the control of their execution?" "In what way are instruments and targets of planning centrally planible?"

Thus, by centralization, different things can be understood: centralization of the capital of the workers; of the flow of goods; of the economic policy decisions or of the means for their implementation. Every centralized decision means the transfer of some activity from the peripheral zone into a center. Centralization always increases the differences between the periphery and the center to the benefit of the latter. The time inevitably comes when these differences increase to the extent of creating a political problem.

D. DECENTRALIZATION

The process of decentralization is the process in which planning decisions are transferred from one center to other centers, be it in a spatial sense (from the capital city to the region) or in a functional sense (from one single planning board to various government departments). The antithesis of centralization, decentralization, does not, however, solve the basic problem of planning, since it only represents a correction in the mechanism of monocentric planning.

(1) Decentralization assumes, as a rule, the pre-existence of a central plan and its methodology which dominates all decisive actions in planning.

(2) It represents only a certain marginal deviation which the center thinks it can afford to permit while remaining the arbiter of the planning process.

(3) Concessions are made in minor matters, considered of secondary

importance following the principle: *de minimis non curat pretor* (the great judge should not be bothered by small matters).

(4) The organs of the center take priority for the central plan, regarding the aims, time and resources, and leave the residuum for decentralized organs. A planning hierarchy exists in which the decentralized planners are always subservient to the central one, however important their aims may be for the population.

III. THE POLYCENTRIC PLANNING MECHANISM

A. BASIC THEORETICAL CHARACTERISTICS

The basic characteristics of polycentric planning that we have developed from our analysis so far are the following:

(a) The polycentric mechanism consists of one open planning mechanism, comprising one set of operations within a national economy (though it can also be extended over several states; nevertheless it is *one* planning mechanism).

(b) This planning mechanism consists of many plans, i.e., there are many planning centers (enterprises, political units, regions, states) which prepare, decide, carry out, and control their plans independently. The polycentric mechanism is composed so that its plans are oligo- and polyplans. Monoplans, which – *ex definitione* – do not take other plans into account, are not compatible with such a mechanism.

(c) With a polycentric mechanism the interrelation between plans is achieved in a competitive or cooperative way, i.e., by a specific planning action optimalizing the targets which will be described later.

(d) We are dealing here with an open, mixed planning mechanism in which elements of the market, administrative, contract, and household mechanisms are retained. The competition goes on not only among plans, but also among various mechanisms. In this sense the planning mechanism is an open mechanism (i.e., open to competition of other mechanisms) with the tendency towards choosing the optimal mechanism for a specific part of the economic process.

Polycentric planning is based on a type of competitive planning having the following characteristics: There is a tendency towards perfect competition among plans (price elasticity $= \infty$); the volume of production is elastic, tending towards maximal satisfaction of consumer demand; prices approach the minimal cost level; the consumers' decisions are autonomous; investments are induced, investment depending on potential gains from planning; the distribution of the product follows the principle of efficiency (in socialist countries: to each according to the productivity of his labor; and workers' management is a logical consequence of this principle); the deflationary tendency stimulates the economic mechanism to rationality in real terms; foreign trade is free, i.e., integrated in the planning mechanism in the same way as internal trade. The planning mechanism is open to foreign competition, tending to minimize the socially necessary labor on an international scale.

B. SPECIFIC AIMS OF POLYCENTRIC PLANNING

Polycentric planning has to solve the problems outlined at the beginning of this paper, as follows:

1. *Macro- and Micro-Planning*

For reasons given above (indivisibility of the factors of production, avoiding risk on the market, increased social interdependence, etc.) modern enterprises must plan. We are here leaving aside the problem of when it is possible for an enterprise to plan, when it is useful, and when it becomes a necessity (an economic law), and of when and where the effects of the market can provide better results than planning. The planning of the enterprise must be based on its independent decisions. Planning in which the enterprise had no initiative, no responsibility, or no risk to carry when fulfilling the plan, could not operate effectively.

Micro-planning is limited by the boundaries of the enterprise, and one should not expect more from it than it can give. There must be a balance between planning resources and planning requirements within the framework of the enterprise as a planning unit. A balanced plan shows the interrelation of the physical use values of the planning targets of enterprises. The technological coefficients are equilibrium points in the mechanism of the micro-planning of the firm. Problems arise when we deal with the integration of the micro-economic operations of the enterprises into a macro-economic (social) plan. The integration effect of the plans of enterprises is more complex than a simple aggregation of their individual microplans, and a macro-planning mechanism has to deal with a much wider range of problems: from those of income redistribution and social cost transfers to evaluation of extra-economic targets. The macroplan can have a greater gain effect in one way and a smaller one in another than a sum of microplans.

The distinction between macro- and micro-economic planning is seen in a whole sequence of secondary and further effects in economic activity: economies of scale; external economies; different multipliers and accelerators, etc. In monocentric planning, linking all economic subjects to the decisions of the Center, such effects are erased and their performance is paralyzed. Polycentric planning endeavors to find a way to let them come to full effect, and to make the planning of such secondary effects possible. Therefore polycentric planning must especially plan to maximize social gains and minimize social waste derived from the activities of independent enterprises. It must comprehend their integrative effect at different macro-economic levels – the commune, the region, the state, the international stage – and the effect on different sectors of industry, on different groups of population, etc. Macro-economic planning with such a mixed planning mechanism cannot confine itself to pure planning in the narrow sense but must especially deal with the combined effect of the market, the firm, and the public agency (which the monocentric plan often leaves aside or simply "does not recognize"). The vast field of social gains and waste provides the ground on which micro-plans are reconciled and compensated by macro-economic planning.

Both a theoretical and a practical solution must be found for this set of problems, and we cannot accept as valid the assumption that the optimal microplans for the enterprise will in principle always be in harmony with the optimal macroplans of society. Such an assumption would simply mean closing one's eyes in the face of the facts, and pretense of solving problems by administrative decree. To assume that relations of this complexity can be successfully solved by a straight command of the government planning authorities is an illusion which is less and less possible the more interdependent the economy is.

2. *Planning in Complex Political Bodies*

A special set of problems arises in connection with the institutional structure of the planning environment in multinational states with a federal constitution, or with regional organizations where political units have the authority to act in planning matters and are not mere geographical areas, i.e., when they have a planning center of their own. Similar problems arise in international planning where several states are involved. To deprive these states or political entities of their authority in matters of planning would mean to greatly reduce their independence, which might be politically impossible to do.

In order to articulate the system of planning in such conditions it is necessary to find a proper place for complex relations in which real economic forces are intertwined with equally real political elements, and this can have a considerable direct effect on planning. It includes the very great possibility of variety in the composition of the organs of planning of all four kinds. Therefore planning theory must find room for such political realities, and organize planning mechanisms which operate in several centers at the same time, and yet cooperate in order to optimize their common gain from planning.

3. *Politicians and Planners*

The relationship between politicians and planners is a subject of special importance in all states where planning is practiced. Planning encompasses such an important part of economic policy that the politicians cannot renounce their decisive role in it. If they did they would lose their social justification. On the other hand, planning is such a complex technical matter that it requires special knowledge and discipline which often politicians do not have, nor are they ready to accept it. This opens up the question of choosing which decisions are politically important and therefore reserved for political bodies to decide upon, and which are politically neutral and therefore can be left to the expert, the planning technician.[1]

On the other hand, in its essence planning is a matter of consistent decisions and consistency is the measure of the internal value of the plan. Political bodies, particularly when the supreme political body – parliament – is in question, are not always willing to accept new obligations which deviate from the traditional procedures of decision making in such bodies. Therefore they are not willing to submit to the principle of consistency. It is a source of conflict between the politocrats and the planocrats. This conflict cannot be solved by authoritarian shortcuts along monocentric lines. It is necessary to seek methods which will preserve the independence of the decisions of the political bodies and at the same time maintain the consistency of the plan. Polycentric planning by its variety of plans and variants of the same plans makes if possible for plans to be more consistent. The more consistent the plans are the easier it is to find objective criteria, since consistency removes a great number

[1] For a more detailed analysis of the relationship between the planners and the politicians, cf. R. Bićanić, "Planificateurs et Politiciens", *Bulletin SEDEIS*, No. 933, Futuribles No. 103 (Paris, Nov. 1, 1965).

of subjective imponderabilia, and imponderabilia are matters which can only be solved by political decisions and not by rationalized (or pseudo-rationalized) expert solutions.

It is particularly important to decide when the planning activity of the planners ceases and when that of the politicians begins, how long it should last and when it should end in the process of preparing the plans, making planning decisions, executing the plans, and in the control of their performance.

To bring the political factor into planning is not easy without falling into the trap of primitive voluntarism. This is particularly so if the plan is presented in one variant only, which cannot be subjected to any changes without interfering with the consistency of the whole plan. Endeavors to attain partial changes of such plans damage both the intervention of the politicians and the consistency of the plan. On the other hand, consistency is often the shield behind which technocrats hide themselves in order to prevent democratization of the planning process. The articulation of plans in several planning centers gives the non-expert element (i.e., the actors outside the technocratic circle of the planning experts) a greater influence on planning. The plans have to become more understandable to the people, both producers and consumers, and to their organizations, in order to be agreed upon and this strengthens the democracy of planning.

4. *Planning in Developing Countries*

Fast-developing countries do not change the institutional structure in all sectors of the economy nor in all economic functions, at the same pace, and therefore show very different degrees of planibility.

To make a consistent plan for heterogeneous economic processes of such diversified dynamics is very difficult if the plan is rigid. What is too great a target for one group, sector, or region, would represent a brake on the development of another. Thus planning at unequal levels of economic development requires different methods, with a different degree of consistency of planning. One planning center is not able, and very often not willing, to meet various demands in a society where different environments and different interests exist, because of the unequal level of development. This also remains valid when class interests are abolished or greatly reduced. If the center of one of such interests proclaims itself as the monocentric bearer of the general national (or social) interest, then the planning mechanism will necessarily be transformed into an authoritarian administrative mechanism, under which increased social and political tensions will be concealed, preventing planning from being successful. At the same time, the market mechanism will necessarily break through all plans, as the monocentric planning mechanism cannot long resist the tension between plans and reality.

In countries that are building socialism by monocentric planning such planning is often mixed with the administrative system of economic management. The question arises to what extent the administrative command dominates the planning mechanism, and to what extent the market mechanism succeeds in resisting or circumventing the grasp of the planners in the first and later stages of planning; to what extent the mechanism of the firm is paralyzed or pushed underground; and how much the mechanism of the household is forced back into self-subsistency.

In the later stages of development, the socialist planning mechanism irresistibly pushes towards liberation from its administrative swaddling bands and monocentric methods. This opens the question whether the stage of authoritarian monocentric planning is really necessary as the first best solution, and if it is, to what extent and at what expense is it necessary. It would require a special study to establish what the economic conditions are under which this occurs and can stand the increasing discrepancies of the second and third best decisions from the economic optimum. Thus a pertinent question must be put to the planners: What price what kind of planning, and how long the optimal period of a specific method of planning lasts. Why must the method be changed and with what effect? In this respect the economic theory of socialist planning has not undertaken much research to work on. But there is no doubt that the move from centralization was not an ideological whim but an economic necessity long overdue.

The process of passing over from the monocentric to the polycentric method of planning in developing countries is carried out by political and economic decentralization; by liberalization of the administrative grip; by setting up a greater number of planning centers; by making the business enterprises more independent; by following the principles of profitableness; by more closely defining the functions of the political and the expert elements; by increasing care for the satisfaction of consumer demands; by removal of voluntarism in planning, particularly in investment decision making; by abolition of the administrative ranking of investment priorities; and by introduction of scientific methods of quantitative analysis in planning, etc.

C. METHODS OF POLYCENTRIC PLANNING

To an authoritarian planner accustomed to commands which he believes will bring about the desired results, polycentric planning may appear to be still more complicated than the market. There is no question of any unnecessary complication but of finding a method of planning which corresponds to modern requirements for accelerated economic development, and to this there can be no simple answer.

The first question to ask is: What would happen if there were no planning mechanism at all? In this case the economy would operate so that individual autonomous decisions would be linked together by a market mechanism, or in certain cases by an administrative or a contract mechanism. The development of the market mechanism of imperfect competition ultimately leads to planning. Market research gives more and more accurate estimates of movements on the market, which necessarily lead to action to remove cyclical and other disturbances by more planning.

With a mixed monocentric planning mechanism all plans are administratively or economically under the domination of one central plan. All other plans are derived from it, with all the consequences of such a monopolistic-monopsonistic situation in which the *formal* compulsory adjustment to plans is paid for by heavy *real* sacrifices. Polycentric planning is meant to avoid such losses. Nevertheless, it has its own problems. What methods can be used to solve the problem of interaction of numerous individual plans in a polycentric planning system? The linking of the plans cannot be left to the market mechanism because by definition we are dealing with a mixed planning mechanism of interlinked competitive or interdependent plans.

The market mechanism plays the important role of a substitute which can replace planning whenever the market gives more net social gain than does planning. This is considered formally impossible in a monocentric mechanism, but actually the market breaks through such plans in spite of prohibitions and the great variety of planning disciplines.

1. *Two Levels of Contact*

The study of economics has not yet reached such a level as to enable a scientifically perfect choice of an optimum overall plan. Experience with formalized planning models is neither very great nor very well verified, and the choice of optimum planning targets based on macro-economic linear programming is still far from being generally applicable. Still less applicable is the method of non-linear programming. Although the application of quite simple formalized planning models can give many worthwhile results, we have, on the whole, to work with planning methods of a limited degree of probability and substitutability. In other words, the solutions foreseen in the plans are competitive and partly empirical. Thus there exists, in a certain sense, a "market" of particular planning targets, within a plan and a "market of plans". We can conceive of every plan as a "product" brought to the market in which the planning resources represent the supply side, and the planning requirements within a plan the demand side.

In our opinion the "market of plans" in mixed polycentric planning – i.e., such competitive planning centers – has to be established on two main levels.

(a) One is that of oligocentric contacts, advocated for political and economic reasons, on an overall state level. It excludes the application of monoplans established with no regard to other plans. In other words the central government's plan also has to be one of the oligoplans. No plans consisting of indisputable targets and overriding priorities should be superimposed by a monocentric planning authority. This does not mean, of course, that all plans are of equal importance, but only that none is exempt from the application of rational and equal criteria in the examination of planning ends and means. Another criterion is that all plans should meet at an equal level, whether they are territorial (e.g., regional) or functional (e.g., plans for national defense, for foreign currency) oligoplans. To this end many heterogeneous central plans would have to be divided into their component parts, which would have to stand on their own merit. The second level of contact of plans is a mixed one of oligo- and polyplans on the regional level. One has to bear in mind that the local or communal plans have not the same dimensions as the national plans; they are not of the same character on a smaller scale, neither are they dealing with residuals. They consist of a different set of equations and variables. An analogy could be found in the theory of foreign trade. Like exports in international trade, the small planning units represent areas of great concentration of outflows, limited to a small number of articles which they produce, and to a dispersion of small inflows. They need a great number of articles in limited quantities from other areas (imports) to meet the demands of the activities of the population, for which they give a great quantity of a small number of products they produce.

The planning resources represent the output the plan gives to the national economy, while the means are inputs the plan requires from the national economy in order to fulfill its targets. The "price" of the plan is achieved when supply and demand meet (inputs equal outputs), when the means necessary to fulfill the planning targets are obtained, i.e., when the wants and the means are balanced.

In micro-economic planning such a price is an expression of the value in money terms, as a competitive, market, or planned price. But it is difficult to establish such a value in macro-economic plans when these are based on physical use values which are not so easy to express adequately in money terms.[2] This is also the reason why the problem of investment and of integration effect is so difficult to solve in planning.

2. *Five Techniques of Planning*

There are several methods for establishing such a planned "price", which is a relative price, i.e., a price which expresses the relations, with the help of a planning mechanism at which the planned resources balance the planned requirements. So far the following methods have been used: (a) empirical or discretionary planning decisions; (b) game theory; (c) national accounting; (d) material balances; (e) the input-output matrix.

(a) The method of *empirical discretionary plans* is the most primitive method of planning, based on *bargaining* and negotiation on all levels by all actors. The "prices" of the plan are then the result of such bargaining, or if an agreement is not reached, administrative decisions may impose the result.

Such methods of planning are characteristic of monocentric planning at the preparatory stage, in the form of various commissions, expert committees, consultations, and personal intervention. But in monocentricity all this is usually shrouded in a veil of secrecy from which all but a select few are excluded. And those few use their monopoly of knowledge according to their own preferences, and personal predilections. Their political responsibility is greatly reduced, as their action is always covered by the ultimate decision of the authoritarian political organs. Such decisions are discretionary, i.e., no reasons need be given, nor are they subject to rational examination, and their elements are often not even known.

From our point of view bargaining and persuasion, agreements, haggling, and struggling are an empirical search for a relative planning

[2] The problem of a difference between the concept of economic and social planning is discussed in another paper.

"price" a "stock exchange of plans" in which every interested participant, who has access to this bargaining, offers his planning resources and states his requirements for the fulfillment of the targets. But the position of actors is uncertain and arbitrary, since the process is not institutionalized and no one knows his rights nor obligations and all are subject to the voluntaristic decisions of the monocentric planner.

Polycentric planning necessarily has to amply use such methods of planning because of the existence of a great number of plans. But it is essential that discretionary decision making find an objective limit in the competition of the plans. The problem is how to rationalize this process of an empirical search for relative prices of planning aims. Instead of the arbitrariness of composition and the loose terms of reference of commissions and committees, this search should have a proper institutionalized basis. Instead of the influence of personal contacts or pressure groups, scientific methods of decision making should be introduced, and empirical bargaining turned into a rational policy of planning.

It is necessary for polycentric planning that such bargaining should be public and institutionalized, that the bodies for bargaining and negotiation should be independent of both the arbitrariness of the planning bureaucracy and the voluntarism of political actors. Their terms of reference should be regulated within the planning mechanism. Polycentricity requires multilateral formal negotiations on an equal footing where persuasion in less formal discussions meets no success. Moreover, macro-planned targets are bound to pass to an ever greater extent from negotiations "marketing" about planned targets to the method of contract planning among planning centers.

(b) The *theory of games* adapted to the mechanism of polycentric planning could help a great deal in the rationalization of such an empirical process, i.e., the search for an optimal strategy for meeting a maximum of the planning targets with a minimum of other people's means, so that in the planning mechanism the aims of one plan represent the means of another plan (circular planning). It appears that only in monocentric planning does no game exist; in fact, it does exist but is not a "true" game in the technical sense, because it is actually played between a central authoritarian planner and a great number of non-identified planners. In polycentric planning the players are institutionalized and identified in much greater number. Here it is evident that the game of one plan depends on the game of all other plans (a characteristic function). In the transition to a reduced form of game such as we propose, further norms of the characteristic function appear, in which nobody will plan if without the plan he can get more than he gets with the plan; neither will he cooperate with plan A if he can gain more from plan B.

Nevertheless there are basic differences between the theory of games on the monopolistic market and that in planning. We are of the opinion that those differences are as follows: planning is a non-nul-sum game because the gain of one partner (plan) is not the loss of another (plan). Planning represents a "true" game because there is no exploitation of the partners in the game; the transparency of the plan is equal on both sides (as different from the market); the random is excluded as much as possible, and it is assumed that the players are acting with most cautious strategy. We have here to add that in planning the question is not one of the profit of the players but of the gain of society (as a fictive player); there is no intention of exploitation of the market for in planning the competitive struggle is specific, and it is assumed that the players (planners) are of equal intelligence. (This assumption is not accepted in monocentric planning.)

(c) National accounting as a method of planning has raised planning to a more scientific and consistent level (double-entry national book-keeping), but it is concerned with planning in the money form only and therefore has a limited effect in the search for relative planned "prices". National accounts give in financial terms a consistent picture of economic transactions between different sectors. Therefore they can also be widely applied in interregional and international polycentric planning. In this case a greater articulation of sectors would be necessary, which must lead to a greater possibility for the consolidation of individual poly-plans into larger block units, and the more complex registration of their mutual transactions. Thus the *ex post* study of the flows and stocks provides a considerable number of elements for planning *ex ante*. National (social) accounting in a reduced form should exist for every macro-economic planning unit (region, commune).[3]

We can imagine polycentric planning operating on the basis of a whole system of social accounts, more or less complex, registering the flows between states, between federal and regional units, districts and communes, as well as between other institutional sectors. Such social accounting would have to be based on the institutional and not on the functional concept of sectors (i.e., dealing with sectors such as business,

[3] The problem of how to relate micro-planning to macro-social accounting is a special but widely studied problem, and so is the study of the relation between material and regional plans.

government, households, etc., and not with production, consumption, saving, etc.).

(d) *Material balances* as a method of planning are able to solve the problem of relative prices better than national accounting, but they are limited only to partial planning for particular commodities (in the product dimension). The allocation of material products to particular users is nothing else than the setting up of relative planning prices (technical coefficients) of the planned targets in the rows of the balance, and searching for the means in the columns. The drawback of this method is that it is lacking the advantage of aggregation.

(e) So far *input-output* tables provide the most accomplished technique of planning, particularly where polycentric planning is concerned. A matrix has no center and therefore is most suitable for polycentric planning. Accordingly the planning initiative (the impulse) can occur theoretically in any cell of the matrix and its effect is necessarily registered and transmitted throughout the whole matrix of the national economy. The high level of consistency of the matrix excludes the arbitrariness of monocentric decisions. The horizontal and vertical links between all sectors forming the matrix also require material connections which cannot be severed without loss, as can be the case in empirical monocentric planning. The coefficients of the input-output matrix are such relative prices of use values of the quantified planning aims as we have already noted.[4]

Polycentric planning would require quite a number of various matrices with a greater-than-four number of gradients. It could not function without a detailed and combined system of interregional and intersectoral matrices, with numerous and articulated sectors and quite a number of regions.

The improvement of the input-output matrices by inclusion of dynamic and spatial coefficients; the combination of such matrices with social accounting; the inclusion of the production and consumption functions in each quadrant of the matrix; all these are gradually leading to more elaborate formalized models of national economies, already similar to a synthetic picture of the "social machinery", with planning being developed into a kind of social engineering (Richard Stone).

Such input-output matrices enable every planning target to be regis-

[4] The special and rather difficult problem of the transformation of such relative shadow or planned prices of one matrix into prices expressed in money terms on a national and international level has been extensively discussed in all countries and particularly in countries of socialist planning.

tered and connected with the national economy as a whole, i.e., to show its integration effect. Such an articulated system of matrices makes it possible for *everybody to plan for all.* By using the appropriate matrix, every planning center can foresee the effect of its targets on all other economic targets, can gather information about means for its aims from all other plans, and can measure the complex effect of its own action. And this is to our mind one of the main postulates for polycentric planning: that every center should plan not only for itself but for all other centers as well. In other words, every individual plan in the process of preparation, decision making, and execution ought to be integrated into the total economic process, following the relative "prices" expressed by the coefficients of the matrix.[5] This speaks against enforced administrative isolation (deprivation of initiative) which is the basis of monocentric planning, and which breaks such interacting links. In other words, polycentric planning has a great advantage over monocentric, in introducing direct horizontal planning links among enterprises, their associations, and commune-to-commune, and region-to-region centers of planning action. This is in addition to vertical lines of planning communications. Its symbol is a matrix and not a pyramid. Monocentric planning recognizes only links of the plans on the vertical line, but never are such links tolerated on the horizontal or diagonal lines.

Of course this does not mean that everybody has to plan totally all his own and other people's activities, for he would be limited to those parts of the plan in which he has an interest. By using reduced input-output matrices (such as proposed by Professor Tinbergen), it is possible to consolidate such tables to the number of rows and columns which are of interest to particular planning centers.

Input-output matrices would also make possible in a technically adequate way the elaboration of a great number of variants of the plan required by political bodies. There would have to be quite a number of such variants, a dozen or so. In this way every planning initiative can be included in the whole complex plan of the national economy, while the consistency of the plan is retained.

The deficiency of the input-output matrix is that it cannot show which attainments of specific targets are optimal *ex ante*; thus it cannot give the choice of optimal plans. But it does give a possibility of verification of ends and means once selected, and of estimating the integration effect.

[5] In fact, every experienced merchant has his empirical nonformalized input-output matrix in his head, or in his "finger tips", when doing business on the market.

In other words, it discovers their relative prices. It is obvious that every table has to have a different set of relative prices and that a special problem arises of how to find relative prices for a whole set of tables.

3. *The Progress of Knowledge*

In the end, while dealing with methods of planning, one must emphasize the progress of statistical methods and of the technique of computers, which have changed not only the quantity but also the quality of solutions to planning problems. Of the great number of changes we underline only three:

(a) New methods and machines make possible a very great number of complex computing operations. In this way it is possible to deal with the large number (e.g., 4,000) of sectors which are embraced by a national economy, to such an extent that almost no economic transaction can pass unnoticed, either in its magnitude or its effect.

(b) The speed of analytical operations has increased to such an extent that the narrowing time lag between the analytic and the operational activity has to a great extent squeezed the period of operational planning in relation to its implementation. Thus the time dimension will gradually be almost wiped out, when the difference between forecasting on the market and the preparation of the plan comes to be based on faster and more accurate forecasting of perspectives.

(c) The complex handling of the economic process allows a qualitative change of planning in the sense that priority of production can give way to priority of consumption, i.e., planning should no longer have to limit itself to allocating what has been produced but can plan to produce what is wanted for consumption. Methods of forward looking planning (from investment – through production – to consumption) and of backward looking planning (from consumption – through production – to investment) can be intertwined into one system. This is also one of the requirements of polycentric planning.

PART III
COMPUTERS: CENTRALIZERS OR LIBERALIZERS

I. THE ROLE OF COMPUTERS AS INSTRUMENTS IN POLYCENTRIC PLANNING

I. There are at least three different approaches to the use of computers in socio-economic planning:

a. We can discuss them from the point of view of the advantages they provide for planning purposes in government agencies (central, regional, and local) [1] and business corporations, enabling these actors in planning to do more work efficiently.

b. We can discuss computers as instruments of power in decision making in the same way as guns or airplanes are discussed as instruments of power in foreign policy. There is little doubt that computers are not such technical, and politically neutral, instruments in social control as some people think. The reason for this is that some people wish to conceal where real power lies, while for others they present an excuse for running away from the true issues. The problem cannot be reduced to a question of who owns or manages the computers, as it can with other means of production. Nor can it be approached as a problem of who has free access to the financial, intellectual or technical resources to use them, because the computers are instrumental in the very process of decision making.

c. Thirdly, computers can be conceived of as instruments in an information system as such, and the questions that then follow are, "Are they masters or servants?" [2] and if so, "Whose masters and whose servants?" Are they made to shape the government of society or to serve it? Do they represent a revolutionary force in society,[3] greater than

[1] Compare U.S. Senate, *Report to the President on the Management of Automatic Data Processing in the Federal Government* (March 4, 1965), Doc. No. 15.
[2] See the 12 questions to ask any computer system in William A. Gill, "Sound Management and Effective Use of Computers in Federal Government", *Computer Automation,* April 1965.
[3] *Cf. Proceedings, Conference,* "Computer Methods on the Analysis of Large Scale Social Systems", p. 180.

the discovery of the steam engine or telegraph or radio? How do they influence the process of decision making in society? Is there a tendency to centralize, i.e., reduce decision making to a smaller number of men in a closed society, or do they enable human society to open up and liberalize and democratize decision making?

In this essay our special concern is to examine the effect of the use of computers in planning. Are they pushing towards monocentric or polycentric planning? On these matters there is, generally speaking, a marked divergence of opinion which may lead to great controversy in the social sciences of the mid-twentieth century.

One school of thought says that central planning is necessary *because* of computers; the other says that it is not necessary for planning to be centralized *because* of computers. Both opinions are advocated by prominent scholars in many countries. The question is one that is widely discussed in some Western, non-planned countries, while in socialist, planned countries it has become a major issue.[4]

d. The line of thought of the first group, that of the centralized planners, runs as follows: the computer can handle a very great volume of information derived from many members of society, and process it in such a way as to find the optimal solution for planned action, and put this optimum into a plan to which specific targets for each group, or even each individual, can be assigned in order to achieve the overall objectives of the plan. Therefore the participation of all actors is limited to the delivery of information to the Central Planner and to the passive fulfillment of the decisions which his computer has found to be optimal. Thus in the name of Science and on the authority of exact scientific method, the will of all actors should be subordinated to computerized decisions reached by the Central Planner. No other centers are considered to be necessary or desirable, as they only impede the computation of the nationally optimal solution. The computer knows what is good for all people.

e. The other school of thought holds that just because the computer can handle a great volume of information and process it so that each element in the overall plan can be evaluated, it is not necessary to have one single center of decision making. The computer system can take into account a great number of active planning centers and compute the optimal solution of their component parts. Thus the computer can

[4] One of the explanations for a revision of the trend in Soviet planning in 1965, tending toward more centralized methods, was that the use of computers makes centralized planning possible, effective and even imperative.

liberalize the decision making process from servitude to one center and yet make the plan work.

II. The many people who think of the computer as a centralizing force in society have in mind that all relevant planning decisions can be made at a single center, based on computerized information process. All other decisions would be derived from this central decision. In our theoretical language this would be a monocentric planning mechanism.

Our intention here is to describe another planning mechanism, a polycentric one, and consider the use on it of computer information systems. The computer information system is considered to be a simulation of the real social process, and so a polycentric planning mechanism must necessarily be reflected in the information system. A polycentric planning mechanism consists of many planning centers and so requires many computer centers also. Such computer centers must be intertied into one computer information system just as the planning centers in polycentric planning are interconnected into one planning mechanism. Now under the impact of the computer system there is a feedback process which causes changes in the polycentric decision making in planning. What changes can we expect in planning from a combination of polycentrism and a computerized information system?

a. A computer center makes it possible to handle a great quantity of information data, which can be collected from a large number of actors and adequately used in planning.[5] This increase of information can make more services available at lesser cost or greater revenue can be

[5] In 1965 the 26 California State Agencies operated 26 separate computers and 10 additional installations. Local government in California had another 39 computer installations. A complete, state wide information system for the state of California will require 8 communication processors, 1 central communication processor, 1 retrieval processor, 1,600 connections to remote stations and 55 multiplexers. There will be 1,015 data flow interfaces, of which 760 horizontal among state agencies (staff to staff or staff to line) and 255 vertical ones, of which 137 upward directed (individuals and business to the state agencies) and 118 downward directed with field offices and local government. But the volume of transactions of the vertical line will extend to 106 million per year while the horizontal line will handle 10 million transactions per year or 10% of the total.

The leading Soviet authority on computers, A. Dorodnitsin, estimated that Soviet planning fully computerized would require 4,000 computers carrying 100,000 operations a second or 10^{16} operations a year. An All Soviet State Operative System of processing economic information would consist of distinct computer centers connected by lines of communication in order to secure a continuous and ramified circulation of information and its diversified analysis. *Pravda,* February 24, 1966.

secured at the same cost. The inclusion of many more actors and much more information is made possible by constructing the information system for the planning mechanism on polycentric lines.

b. The information collected and processed by the computer gives better quality information based not only on new data, but also new usage of old data. This increases the knowledge of social interdependence, which necessarily leads to a decline in the functions of the command mechanism. When every actor in planning can establish for himself his position in the socio-economic system there is no need for the existence of a central organ of command whose function it is to assign every actor his role, and allocate to him the goods and services needed so that he can perform his planned function.

In such a system of information which reduces discretionary decisions it is possible to make greater use of prediction models, take timely action to remove disequilibria, thus making deviations from planned objectives smaller. This means that the role of the central planner as arbitrary decision maker is largely rendered superfluous in favour of planning models, parameters of planning action and other instruments.

c. The computer has very great speed in handling information relevant to planning. Therefore it can bring the plan closer to those who implement it. Or, to be more precise, the planning cycle of preparation, decision, implementation and evaluation can be greatly shortened. The gestation period of the plan can be reduced, the decisions of planners can be communicated faster to those whose role it is to implement them, etc. Speedy cognizance of interdependence would reduce the scope and range of conflict among planning actors and therefore make imperative decisions of the central planner redundant, and consistency among planned objectives and decisions of many centers easier to achieve.

d. The great memorizing capacity of the computer system can be used for forecasting and prediction of future trends in planning and replace the voluntaristic and arbitrary choice of strategic decisions in planning made by the central planner.[6]

e. The existence of a mechanism of many planning centers interlinked by a system of computer centers would change the traditional hierarchical administrative order of communication. Direct cross-section information among various planning centers, without the interference of

[6] The Californian federation of computers will have a capacity to store 36 milliard characters. It will memorize 100 data of personal information for each inhabitant of California. It will take 5-10 years to translate existing data and memorize them into a system of retrievable information.

central bureaucracy would be brought into being. This would enhance the existing jurisdiction of various government agencies and make possible new, more democratic forms of administrative ties. Moreover, the federated computer system would make actors in planning more responsible and autonomous in their action than in the classical mechanism of information because of the great number, variety and speed of operations on which their decisions will have to be based.

f. A computer system of information puts all planning actors, those in the central government as well as those in the smallest communal unit and business enterprise, potentially in a position to make use of the same quantity and quality of information relevant to planning. It can be acquired at almost the same moment with almost the same speed. Therefore other things being made equal the quality of decisions can be on an equal level. Moreover, those planners who are closer to implementation in the field can enjoy information from direct personal observation as well as the universal information collected and processed for planning purposes. In this information system the closer planners are to direct producers the more they can enjoy such specific advantages over planners removed from actual operations.[7]

g. Awareness of *social interdependence* expressed in quantitative terms which forms the basis of every plan makes the coordination of the autonomous planning actions more possible among government agencies themselves and between them and business enterprises. Social interdependence makes it possible for a great number of actors to plan without losing their identity, in order to combine individual initiative and use the best opportunity on the one hand, and the responsibility of acting as one autonomous unit of planning on the other.

h. The computer system makes the *comparability* of planning objectives more effective and the measurement of achievements more refined. Therefore the intervention of central planners in the planning process is not important as it is in a monocentric system, where the measurement is crude and slow, and the rules of comparability arbitrarily imposed.[8]

[7] An I.B.M. manager said: "By computer-centered, I do not mean centralized operations. Companies will have a computer center where all the corporate data are instantly reflected. However, there will also be decentralized locations – I think we must have decentralized management to get the best out of people – where all will be able to operate on the same data. The net result will be a more effective decentralized operation because the conflict of different data has been eliminated." Cf., *Automation and the Middle Manager*, p. 23. (American Foundation on Automation and Employment Inc., New York.)

[8] These two elements are built into any system of monocentric planning since they can, at will, separate the costs from the price, and the propensity to invest

In possession of such objective comparability of planning action and the evaluation of its implementation a system of polycentric planning can operate more effective than a monocentric one.

All these properties of the computer change the quality of planning and make it possible in fields of human activity where it previously was considered impracticable. On the whole the computer can make planning, be it macro-economic or micro-economic, a scientific operation and minimize its voluntaristic (authoritarian) and empirical character.

How do these properties of the computer affect the dilemma of monocentric versus polycentric planning? In the first place, the greater amount of information collected in one place by the computer has considerable effect on planning. The greater the amount of information, the greater the possibility of combination in planning, the greater the degree of freedom of the planners, and the greater the possibility of involving more people in the process. The second effect of computerized information is that it eliminates a number of intermediaries, and in this sense appears to make the process more centralized.

At the same time, a consequence of this change is that it increases both the role of the central planner and the role of the first actor, who is the prime emitter of information. The assumption that the central planner is rationally and objectively better informed about the facts relevant for planning is not valid because (a) the information received does not necessarily reflect the real situation but is limited by the predetermined idea of the central planner who selects and defines the information he wants to receive. If left to himself the central planner is the person farthest removed from the terrain and therefore is not in a good position to evaluate the information he is receiving. Also, (b) the first emitter of planning information is in a position to decide for himself the way in which he will provide the required information to the central planner. Thus the question arises, to what extent is it in his interest to deliver the information which is vital in planning activity to the central planner? Or, in other terms, what is the optimum degree to which he will be most interested in supplying the best possible information?

The assumption that all information in planning is accurate is not realistic, as is shown by the experience of all countries where planning is practiced. Therefore the problem of information avoidance and information evasion is pertinent (inaccurate or false reporting, double

---

and to consume in personal consumption depends on their decision (in short and middle term plans). Nothing in the system forces them to comply with a speedy and exact system of measurement.

planning, concealing of reserves, understating of targets, etc.). In monocentric planning this problem is incomparably more difficult to solve than in polycentric planning which brings the planning decision closer to the first emitter, i.e., the direct producer or consumer. In other words, the question in planning is how to make the prime information emitter interested enough to deliver accurate information.

Another aspect of centralized information collection by the computer refers to what is being done with the data, i.e., the problem of dissemination of information. This is a highly political question which depends partly on to whom the results of the computerized information are passed after being processed. If the data are not disseminated but are retained by the central planner, who keeps a monopoly of that knowledge for himself, then he obviously enjoys exclusive benefit from the knowledge of the information supplied by the computer.

The processing of information by the computer, in its classification, articulation and ramification, makes the selection of important data more objective, thus making the strategy of planning less dependent on decisions of one center and one model. Instead of thinking in terms of concentric circles or of a social pyramid one is led to think in terms of social matrices, which makes the awareness of social interdependence of many centers more acute, and dependence on the decisions of one supreme center superfluous. In monocentric planning such interdependence is represented as dependence on one center, not on the interdependence of centers upon each other, which is the characteristic of polycentric planning. Ignorance and unawareness of inter-dependence is one of the main justifications or excuses for the existence of monocentric planning. It is the command of those who know, in the name of knowledge over ignorance, or the disregard of planned interdependence. The computers, by spreading the knowledge of interdependence over many centers, enable the actors in these centers to find their optimal places in polycentric planning. Moreover, they make possible a greater ramification of the plans (variants) on the one hand, and a greater aggregation of many particular plans on the other.

The speed of processing planning data makes it possible to include in the planning procedure a great number of actors who make decisions almost at the very moment when their information is acquired; this allows coordination and integration of decisions. By reducing the time lag between the process of preparing the plan, making the decision over the planning targets, and better control of the planning process while it is being implemented, the character of the plan is altered in the sense that the role of one command center is minimized. Decisions can be made on the spot and rapidly integrated.

All feedback effects incorporating and correcting the decisions of many centers can be quickly recorded and dealt with without the overriding role of the authoritarian central planner. The one-way traffic of monocentric planning can easily be turned into a two- or multi-way traffic of polycentric planning.

The depersonalization of planning decision making leads to the replacement of the men who command by the machine which serves. The computer can give only what is fed into it. The machine depends on what actors who control it want to get out of it. This applies also to the problem of monocentricity or polycentricity of planning. The computer can work out such plans as those who manipulate it are ready and willing to provide for the computerized society, i.e., for those who know and are willing to make use of this powerful instrument of social decision making.

III. Under what conditions can we expect those tendencies to prevail in the development of computer information systems which benefit polycentric planning? We shall divide our further discussion of the problem into three parts. First we shall discuss the organizational problems of computer centers in polycentric planning. Then we shall proceed to examine the technical conditions under which there are advantages for polycentric planning. And finally we shall consider the social implications of an information system in such a polycentric planning mechanism as a public service.

II. THE DECISION MAKING PROCESS AND THE COMPUTER INFORMATION SYSTEM IN POLYCENTRIC PLANNING

We start this part of our deliberation with two general statements:

Decisions should be separated from information.
Centralization should not be confused with rationalization and generalization.

The relationship between decision making and information processing is not direct. A centralized system of information can provide information for a decentralized system of decision making (We are talking here of a system of polycentric not monocentric information).[1] It is true that all decisions depend on information, but that also means, not on any particular piece of information, but on a multitude of it. The better the quality and quantity of information the wider the basis for decisions in planning and the freer the planners. The decision making process consists of information and also the sifting of the relevant from the non-relevant according to the planning aims. This, in its turn implies value judgements.

Centralization is often considered to be identical with generalization and rationalization. Centralization in planning means the transfer of the decisions to one single decision making actor, individual or collective, whose will decides about the action of all other actors. Generalization, on the contrary, means the acceptance of certain rules of action by an ever greater number of people. Centralization emphasizes the difference between the center and the periphery. Generalization implies homo-

[1] A survey conducted among big American corporations showed at the widespread opinion among managers that "a more rapid and complete centralization of information, but not necessarily changed locales for decision making, will result from advanced computerization". . . . "Hierarchy will become much flatter (read polycentric – R. B.) with fewer levels, and much more delegation of decisions, formerly made at higher levels of responsibility, to lower levels" . . . "there will be a greater degree of centralization in information gathering, but not necessarily in the decision making process." *Automation and the Middle Manager*, pp. 22, 23, 40.

genization which erases such differences. Thus generalization of an information system does not necessarily mean that all information has to be collected, processed and retrieved in one place, according to the will of one central actor only. A generalized system of information, as we understand it, is one where all people take part in the supply and use of information.

The process of rationalization, in the sense of minimization of means for given ends, does not necessarily mean that all that is central is rational. Rationality depends on the principle of ratio, and this principle can be chosen in many different ways.

Therefore we must reject the assumption that all processes of centralization necessarily represent rationalization or generalization. The imperfections of centralization have their price, and to the question "What price decentralization?" the retort is "What price centralization?"

A polycentric mechanism of planning requires many decision making centers depending on different levels, size, kind, capacity and volume of information. The cyclical process of the preparation of the plan, decision making, implementation and evaluation depends on a great variety of information. Therefore the process of simulation of such a mechanism by an information system must necessarily consist of different kinds of the hardware and software of the computer system. In any activity so complex as the modern economy different sizes, types and makes of computers must be used. A great variety of personnel is also needed, with very different training, computer language used and volume of material handled for very varying purposes.[2] The specific feature of polycentric planning is the existence of many planning centers of decision making which intercommunicate their information not only on a vertical, hierarchical line, but also on a horizontal link of mutual interties on an equal footing. Channels of information must be left open to operate without the interference of the Central Planner, and independently of him. These centres must be able to talk directly to each other and develop planning action on the basis of their own decisions. The social integration of such a system is greater than in a centralized system as the ties among different actors are not dependent on the channels connecting them with one center only. They are interwoven into a network of information

[2] A. Dorodnitsin underlined the difference between the computers used in scientific research which process a small number of figures (several dozens to several tens of thousands in certain rare cases). Economic computations have to handle original information consisting of several tens and hundreds of millions of figures and words which have to be processed into an output of some documents of finite size instead of infinite analysis of numbers. *Pravda*, Feb. 24, 1966.

which secures a much thicker fabric of mutual interaction. A system of polycentricity of information centers must correspond to a mechanism of polycentricity with many planning centers.[3]

[3] For example the California statewide system of information proposes a Federation of Organizational Computer Centers tied together by an Information Central and operating within a framework of compatibility rules subject to a few basic constraints.

"A basic conclusion is that independent geographically distinct information processing centers in California State and local government should be integrated without being necessarily physically consolidated ... the system should be developed to allow separate centers to 'talk with each other'. Additionally, each processing center must be able to understand all others either through language standardization or translation." "The Information Central is a computer based system giving semi-autonomous, computer centers an automated means for exchanging information ..." This Central will not store data but only the location of data requested – it will centralize information about information. *California Statewide Information System*, Study, Lockheed missiles and spare Co., 1965, pp. 2-5, 2-7.

III. TECHNICAL REQUIREMENTS

The second question concerning the operation of a polycentric system of information is that of technical requirements. If intercommunication of computer centers is envisaged there must be a common language of intercommunication. But because there must be a minimum of technological compatibility among these centers this does not mean that they ought to be centrally run.

As far as the hardware is concerned intercommunication must be possible so that they can transmit, process and store information. But it is not necessarily for them to be technically uniform or centrally directed in order to achieve this. The minimum requirement is limited to their structural technical compatibility and mutual adjustment. Direct wire connections do not mean monopoly of processing information data by one center. Centers can, and do, have a considerable portion of their time for their own use according to their own interests, initiative and objectives, and this they can use better on their own than when commanded by some overriding authority. The possibility of using replaceable computers in both directions makes the system flexible and adaptable to varied needs of comprehensive planning.[1] The centers must be able to understand each other by using the computer language and the code common to the system presented in a comparable format. Even if different computer languages are in use their compatibility is enough to make the system operate successfully.[2]

[1] This has led some experts such as John R. Price, the "father of Telstar" to formulate the guiding principle of future development as *technological integration and physical decentralization* of society through a universal system of communication by satellites, microwaves, wave guides and laser beams.

[2] The Federated System with an Information Central as its nerve center will require less standardization than a completely centralized system. Nevertheless compatibility is part of the price for integrating a number of diverse operating systems into a larger system (codes, language and calaloguing techniques, files). However the Federated System gives freedom of choice in computer equipment,

Technical experts developing a computer system for general use in public administration [3] had to solve the problem of a central versus a decentralized computer system, and they have described the advantages of the two systems in the following way:

In the matter of *hardware* (computers, consoles, retrieving systems etc.)

a. A central system has advantages when different users are in proximity. When the users operate at greater than optimal distances a decentralized system of computers is preferable.

b. When dealing with similar processing needs a centralized system of computers has advantages. When comprehensive tasks have to be performed with many diversified processing operations a decentralized system is better, which makes possible not only a diversification of processing methods but also specialization of different machines.

c. Where work is complementary so that the cumulative load is evenly distributed over time a centralized system can operate satisfactorily. When peaks in load have to be dealt with in specific operations and no complementarity appears but each operation has peaks at the same time as others (e.g. in a planning cycle) a decentralized system of a greater number of computers has advantages over the centralized one.

d. If the requirements of one organization fully match the load capacity of one machine established for that special purpose a centralized (one machine – one organization) system has advantages over a decentralized. If more load is required than one machine can handle at a time large computers are more suitable. The economy of scale is advantageous and large computers can handle more load from a greater number of organizations.

e. Large machines attract work from a great number of smaller organizations and therefore perform a centralizing effect on them due to economy of scale.[4] On the other hand if the need for additional processing is supplemented by large machines operating for a greater number of recipients a decentralized system has precedence. Comparatively small organizations can each have their own computer normally used to full capacity. For extra loads they can engage additional machines which

---

selection and data processing methods to individual participating units. *California Statewide Information System Study*, pp. 2-11.

[3] Compare "Centralization v. Decentraliation", *ibid.*, 5-8, 5-11.

[4] This surplus capactiy was very significant in extending the use of computers from natural to social sciences and to educational purposes.

operate within a larger system offering their services for which they are available at different times.[5]

When considering *software* (files of information):

a. A centralized system makes the storage of redundant information once only. In a decentralized system it is possible that data will be stored in two or more places which is more expensive. This turns into an advantage when the necessity for specialization, secrecy and physical security are considered, and the storage of data in one place only can prove to be risky in the case of some natural or other disturbance.

b. When the users operate in close proximity the costs of retrieving information are smaller and usage of more than one processing machinery can be wasteful. If, on the contrary, the distance is great in space or there is diversified function software is better utilized on the spot and only final data can be processed to various terminals. This is valid when communication costs (teletyped transfer communications) exceed the cost of storage of redundant data.

c. The greater capacity of a central computer can secure more service, but it may remain idle from time to time. A decentralized system of composite data processing can better divide the load and utilize computer services more efficiently.

d. One central computer operates mainly on the principle of uniformity of use, dealing with averages and norms. A decentralized system can use particular systems of information adapted to diversified needs. The language can be adapted to specialized requirements, and specific codes for recording developed. This technological analysis favours a decentralized information system for great social systems and for their diverse tasks such as polycentric planning. Besides the principle of "centralized information and decentralized decision", – and on the top of it – stands another principle, that of technical decentralization and social integration, which does not mean centralization.

[5] Larger computers operate like indivisible power stations in an electric power system.

IV. INFORMATION UTILITY AS PUBLIC SERVICE

If it is technically possible, indeed preferable, to organize a computerized information service how is this likely to affect two other constraints on planning? i.e. is planning economically feasable, does it pay, or secure more gain than waste, and is it politically preferable, does it affect those in control of political power.

We shall approach this problem here from the restricted point of view of polycentric planning versus monocentric. The problem relates to the social function of computers and to what extent their services are socialified.[1] This must be considered in light of the four functions of the computer system: to collect information, process it, store it and retrieve it.

We are leaving aside the problem of how much greater volume of information a computer, or system of computers can handle for the operator. Nor shall we deal here with the problem of who should own the computer, i.e. the advantages of ownership or renting of the computer etc.

The first extension of the individual computer service beyond the private use of the operator was in selling free time, from which fallout effect many educational and research institutions benefited and the social sciences made great use. Soon a commercial service came into being selling time to others who requested it as a surplus time sharing proposition. At the present moment an ever increasing use of computer services is spreading which goes beyond the mere commercial selling of surplus services. The computer service is becoming an information utility, and it is looked at in this way in many quarters.

[1] We are using the term *socialification* instead of the more familiar socialization partly because the latter has several different meanings in law, psychology, sociology and economics, partly to avoid the political tag. The term is intended to describe the extension of the use of the computer in a process of social interdependence beyond the internal organizational interests of the operator.

The computer system of government and information agencies is growing into a public utility information service (note the influence of the Bureau of the Budget regarding the use of computers in the U.S.). Similar ideas have also spread to those who specialize in organizing a regular computerized information service for business forecasting scientific research consultants, commercial air traffic, weather control, political election predictions etc. There are several reasons why a commercial service is turning into an information utility with public responsibilities.

Although the process is still in the early stages of development we feel the following to be the main causes of the tendency:

a. Accessibility. The problem of accessibility can be looked at from several angles: *technical* accessibility or the possibility of making use of the computer services by having physical access to them; *financial* accessibility, i.e. the means to pay for the use of the services; *personal* accessibility, acquiring the knowledge of the usefulness of the computer and breaking the resistance of the old administrative managers who are afraid of innovations and feel insecure before problems which computers bring. There are also *political* problems of accessibility, similar to those in other media of mass communication.

It is in the public interest that computer services should be as widespread as possible because of the great advantages such services bring to those who can make use of them, and because of the many monopolistic privileges that develop among those who have interest to limit access. The polycentric mechanism provides a useful means to break up monocentric privileges.[2]

By meeting the requests of the many in polycentric planning a computer information system develops a coalescence of purposes of individual organizations, public and private, and new needs are created to be satisfied.

[2] In Great Britain the government is establishing a National Computer Center with the aim of providing users with a catalogue of computer programs already available in Britain, to encourage the development of programs with similar requirements, and to spread the use of and research into computer services. One of the effects of this national computer service is expected to be not only the expansion of the use of computers, but the break up of the monocentricity of existing computer centers. In both cases, the linking of existing computer centers and services will enable the community of decision making centers to make greater and more effective use of computers. This will be done by increasing polycentricity of information systems.

b. The technology of the computer information service requires, as we have seen, the technical compatibility of various kinds of hard and software through the polycentric system. Public regulation is needed to secure these beyond the limits of private interests.

c. The computerized information system can only operate effectively on the basis of a great volume of information collected and stored. This can only be done if the "natural" limits of information bound by the private interests of the firm or the boundaries of jurisdication of the public agency can be overcome. This can be achieved on the basis of contractual or public regulation, and the duty to supply information and the right to use it must be effectively established. This is of greater importance in a polycentric than in a monocentric mechanism because of its complexity. An analogy can be made here with the use of statistical public service, technological standards, book-keeping regulations, accountancy etc.[3] Such an information system can be developed properly on a generalized public utility basis, which makes collecting and retrieving of information a public service.

d. An information system based on computers raises many legal problems their specific characteristic being the great speed with which a large volume of complete and vital information can be retrieved. Problems concerning *personal* privacy require specific treatment and legal protection. *Business* activities from patent rights and business secrets up to unfair competition must be considered. A third field that will need attention is that of *government* agencies covering the field of publicity of information, state secrets, classified information etc.

At present the era of computers has just begun, and large corporations, big university institutes and central government agencies are those who have learned to use the services of the computers. (These are in the position of a machine gun team fighting a tribe of archers.) In this sense the computers act predominantly as individual monopolistic centers of decision making. Their capacity is sold or hired only as a secondary service to particular customers. One can envisage the time when, besides

[3] The obligation to provide information is linked directly to the use of services in commercial information systems, e.g. the I.B.M. information service requests all firms utilizing their marketing information service to accept the obligation to provide a considerable amount of information about their own marketing which is subsequently entered into the I.B.M. information model in order to improve it.

individual computers, there will be a system of computers as a public and social service, making their use available to all, as, for instance, statistical or public library services are today.[4]

[4] The history of knowledge shows that libraries, which were private and have become public, were linked in most advanced countries into one system by an overall catalogue service and by the organization of lending services. So far nobody has had the idea of transferring all books to one place or of disposing of them from one single center. The same applies to the telephone service, which started as private telephones and later was developed into a public service through the organization of local exchanges linked together all over the country. Later on, the system of direct contact was introduced which enables every telephone subscriber to dial any other subscriber without asking the distributing services of the exchange personnel or the permission of the central exchange. In this case, again, the technique of progress has replaced the role of the central distributer. This is how we envisage the development and role of the computers in modern society, i.e., as a polycentric public social service. Its implications for the democratization and liberalization of the planning process are of utmost importance.

These ideas have already found concrete technical application in public administration. One of the largest firms, the Lockheed missile and space business firm in the United States, proposed to the State Governor of California the establishment of a federation of computer centers, both state and local, tied together by an information center. This center would spread information on a state-wide basis as a central electronic index of data stored in the files of the participating computer centers. This organization of centers would supply the state administration, the courts and the business and government sectors with a skills inventory file for state employees, information about population trends and forecasts of further developments, government economic policies, activities affecting business, and analysis of consumer behavior, all of which could be made available to the business community. Cf. *Christian Science Monitor*, November 2 and December 27, 1965.

In Great Britain the government is establishing a National Computer Center with the aim of providing users with a catalogue of computer programs already available in Britain, to encourage the development of programs with similar requirements, and to spread the use of and research into computer services. One of the effects of this national computer service is expected to be not only expansion of the use of computers, but the breaking up of the monocentricity of existing computer centers. In both cases, the linking of existing computer centers and services will enable the community of decision making centers to make greater and more effective use of computers. This will be done by breaking current monopolies and increasing the polycentricity of decision making.

INDEX

PUBLICATIONS OF THE INSTITUTE OF SOCIAL STUDIES, THE HAGUE

SERIES MAIOR

1. S. N. Eisenstadt: *Essays on Sociological Aspects of Political and Economic Development*. 1961. 88 pp. Dglds. 10.—

2. C. A. O. van Nieuwenhuijze: *Society as Process: Essays in Social Sciences Method*. 1962. 281 pp. Cloth. Dglds. 28.—

3. J. A. Ponsioen (ed.): *Social Welfare Policy*. First Collection: *Contribution to Theory*. 1962. 287 pp. Cloth. Dglds. 25.—

4. J. A. Ponsioen: *The Analysis of Social Change Reconsidered: A Sociological Study*. 1962. 17 pp. Cloth. Dglds. 14.—

5. C. A. O. van Nieuwenhuijze: *Cross-Cultural Studies*. 1963. 289 pp. Cloth. Dglds. 28.—

6. George Kurian: *The Indian Family in Transition: A Case Study of Kerala Syrian Christians*. 1961. 147 pp., map. Dglds. 15.—

7. Marion W. Forrester: *Kenya To-Day: Social Prerequisites for Economic Development*, 179 pp., 2 maps. Cloth. Dglds. 15.—

8. Zimmerman, L. J. (ed.): *Economic Planning*. 1963. 144 pp., 8 figs. Cloth. Dglds. 18.—

9. J. A. Ponsioen (ed.): *Social Welfare Policy*. Second Collection: *Contributions to Methodology*. 1963. 178 pp. Cloth. Dglds. 20.—

10. E. de Vries (ed.): *Essays on unbalanced growth: A Century of Disparity and Convergence*. 1962. 221 pp. Cloth. Dglds. 24.—

11. C. A. O. van Nieuwenhuijze (ed.): *Markets and Marketing as Factors of Development in the Mediterranean Basin*. Papers presented at the Second Assembly of the Mediterranean Social Sciences Research Council held at Cairo, December 1-4, 1962. 1963. 153 pp. Cloth. Dglds. 16.—

MOUTON & CO · PUBLISHERS · THE HAGUE

Bei Fragen zur Produktsicherheit wenden Sie sich bitte an:
If you have any questions regarding product safety,
please contact:

Walter de Gruyter GmbH
Genthiner Straße 13
10785 Berlin
productsafety@degruyterbrill.com